Neuropsychological Assessment in Clinical Child Psychology

DEVELOPMENTAL CLINICAL PSYCHOLOGY AND PSYCHIATRY SERIES

Series Editor: **Alan E. Kazdin,** *Western Psychiatric Institute*

In the Series:

Neuropsychological Assessment in Clinical Child Psychology

George W. Hynd

Volume 16.
Developmental Clinical Psychology and Psychiatry

SAGE PUBLICATIONS
The Publishers of Professional Social Science
Newbury Park   Beverly Hills   London   New Delhi

For information address:

SAGE Publications, Inc.
2111 West Hillcrest Drive
Newbury Park, California 91320

SAGE Publications Inc.
275 South Beverly Drive
Beverly Hills
California 90212

SAGE Publications Ltd.
28 Banner Street
London EC1Y 8QE
England

SAGE PUBLICATIONS India Pvt. Ltd.
M-32 Market
Greater Kailash I
New Delhi 110 048 India

Printed in the United States of America

Library of Congress Cataloging-in-Publication Data

Hynd, George W.
  Neuropsychological assessment in clinical child psychology.

  (Developmental clinical psychology and psychiatry; v. 16)
  Bibliography: p.
  Includes index.
  1. Neuropsychological tests for children.
2. Pediatric neuropsychology. I. Title. II. Series.
[DNLM: 1. Neuropsychological Tests—in infancy & childhood. 2. Neuropsychology—in infancy & childhood.
3. Psychophysiology—in infancy & childhood.
W1 DE997NC v.16 / WM 145 H997n]
RJ486.6.H96 1988 618.92′80475   88-3222
ISBN 0-8039-3004-6
ISBN 0-8039-3005-4 (pbk.)

FIRST PRINTING 1988

CONTENTS

SERIES EDITOR'S INTRODUCTION

Interest in child development and adjustment is by no means new. Yet, only recently has the study of children benefited from advances in both clinical and scientific research. Advances in the social and biological sciences, the emergence of disciplines and subdisciplines that focus exclusively on childhood and adolescence, and greater appreciation of the impact of such influences as the family, peers, and school have helped accelerate research on developmental psychopathology. Apart from interest in the study of child development and adjustment for its own sake, the need to address clinical problems of adulthood naturally draws one to investigate precursors in childhood and adolescence.

Within a relatively brief period, the study of psychopathology among children and adolescents has proliferated considerably. Several different professional journals, annual book series, and handbooks devoted entirely to the study of children and adolescents and their adjustment document the proliferation of work in the field. Nevertheless, there is a paucity of resource material that presents information in an authoritative, systematic, and disseminable fashion. There is a need within the field to convey the latest developments and to represent different disciplines, approaches and conceptual views to the topics of childhood and adolescent adjustment and maladjustment.

The Sage Series on *Developmental Clinical Psychology and Psychiatry* is designed to serve uniquely several needs of the field. The Series encompasses individual monographs prepared by experts in the fields of clinical child psychology, child psychiatry, child development, and related disciplines. The primary focus is on developmental psychopathology which refers broadly here to the diagnosis, assessment, treatment, and prevention of problems that arise in the period from infancy through adolescence. A working assumption of the Series is that understanding, identifying, and treating problems of youth must draw on multiple disciplines and diverse views within a given discipline.

The task for individual contributors is to present the latest theory and research on various topics, including specific types of dysfunction, diagnostic and treatment approaches, and special problem areas that affect adjustment. Core topics within clinical work are addressed by the Series. Authors are asked to bridge potential theory, research and clinical practice, and to outline the current status and future directions. The goals of the Series and the tasks presented to individual contributors are demanding. We have been extremely fortunate in recruiting leaders in the field who have been able to translate their recognized scholarship and expertise into highly readable works on contemporary topics.

The present book, authored by Dr. George W. Hynd, is devoted to *Neuropsychological Assessment in Clinical Child Psychology*. The book conveys the role of neuropsychological assessment in the context of child development and clinical work. The discussion is broad and conveys the purposes, advantages, and limitations of neuropsychological assessment. The book presents cross-disciplinary developments in elaborating brain-behavior relationships and historical developments leading to contemporary work. Current research and theory and sources of controversy are presented in an even-handed fashion. For clinical assessment, an eclectic model is provided to encourage the evaluation of diverse neuropsychological abilities and functions in a clinically feasible manner. Commonly used assessment batteries and individual tests are concisely presented and evaluated. Overall, Dr. Hynd has been extremely successful in elaborating the interrelations of test performance, brain functioning, psychological processes, and clinical impairment. It is to his credit and to our benefit that his exceptional scholarship has been complemented with an engaging writing style.

> —*Alan E. Kazdin, Ph.D.*
> Series Editor

PREFACE

While expertise in clinical child neuropsychology conveys to others expectations of competencies relative to assessment and diagnosis, it may be more appropriate to view such expertise as best representing an integrative perspective on brain-behavior relations in children and adolescents. At its most sophisticated level, clinical acumen in neuropsychology represents the conviction that the boundary distinguishing neurology and the behavioral sciences is dynamic and interactive. This is the perspective from which this volume was written.

This book is intended for those embarking on the pursuit of specialized education and supervised training in clinical child neuropsychology. Since the appraisal of the integrity of brain-behavior relations is the most significant and visible service provided by clinicians with such competencies, this volume was prepared in order to provide an overview of contemporary assessment procedures and practices.

Two convictions guided the development of this book. First, it is clear that our current knowledge regarding brain-behavior relations evolved significantly from the work of those interested in behavioral neurology. Thus, one finds a historical perspective which serves to illustrate how our current conceptualizations matured. The historical perspective is believed important since many of the issues so central to our understanding today were first clearly articulated a little over a century ago. Moreover, our ideas have not withstood the test of time and represent a rapidly evolving conceptualization of how our nervous system develops and is reflected in our behavior. Second, it is recognized that objectively measured behavior in children, or indeed in adults, reflects at best indices of the integrity of the central nervous system. Consequently, the standardized and age-normed appraisal of individual differences in children and adolescents emerges as vitally important in distinguishing normal from deviant patterns of behavior.

Consistent with the foregoing is the notion that the objective and well-prepared clinician is more accurate in appraising the integrity of the central nervous system than any single test or test battery. The procedures and instruments of appraisal discussed in this volume should only be viewed as the tools by which clinicians demonstrate their knowledge and mastery of an integrated neurobiological-developmental perspective on the range and course of human behavior.

—George W. Hynd
Athens, Georgia

ACKNOWLEDGMENTS

This volume was written with the assistance of a number of individuals. Dora Ervin's typing was, as always, exceptional. Peg Semrud-Clikeman helped considerably by reading and editing the chapters. Alison Lorys-Vernon provided very helpful editorial comments as well. Dr. Mary Gail Becker, Department of Educational Psychology, Pennsylvania State University, was helpful in developing Appendices A and B. Dr. S. H. Greenblatt, Division of Neurological Surgery, Medical College of Ohio and Dr. Edwin A. Weinstein of Bethesda, Maryland, provided many helpful comments on draft versions of chapters two and three. I am most grateful to all these friends and colleagues for their time and assistance.

Permission is also acknowledged to reprint material appearing in chapters one, four, and five from G. W. Hynd, J. Snow, & M. G. Becker (1986), "Neuropsychological Assessment in Clinical Child Psychology," in B. Lahey & A. Kazdin (Eds.), *Advances in Clinical Child Psychology* (vol. 9), New York: Plenum Publishing Corporation; and for material appearing in chapter six from G. W. Hynd & M. Cohen (1983), *Dyslexia: Neuropsychological Theory, Research and Clinical Differentiation*, New York: Grune & Stratton, Inc.

To Naomi, Without Whom So Much
Would Not Have Been Possible

1

CLINICAL CHILD NEUROPSYCHOLOGY

As brain sciences advance in sophistication, an exclusively behavioral perspective becomes decreasingly tenable and increasingly self-defeating . . . . The discipline of neuropsychology embodies a concerted attempt to relate behavioral variables to brain mechanisms. The approach has had its spectacular successes . . . . We now know much about which part of the brain controls what, about how behavior disassembles under the impact of focal brain lesions, and how cognitive processors interrelate.

—Kinsbourne, 1988

Neuropsychological assessment with children is increasingly becoming a desired, if not expected, service to be performed by clinical child psychologists. Unlike traditional psychological assessment with children, neuropsychological assessment encompasses many different techniques and serves a different purpose (Gaddes, 1980; Hynd & Obrzut, 1981; Taylor, Fletcher, & Satz, 1984). Generally, the purpose of neuropsychological assessment with pediatric patients is to differentiate children whose disorders are either functional or organic, to document the extent of neuropsychological involvement and, in organic conditions, to chart the temporal interactions between ongoing development and recovery or deterioration of function. In response to this increased need for neuropsychological assessment with children, several standardized batteries are available, complemented by a host of ancillary techniques and procedures.

The proliferation of these standardized batteries and techniques should allow psychologists to derive more empirically based statements regarding brain-behavior relations. Thus, through the application of these procedures and standardized techniques, erroneous conclusions as to brain-behavior relations can be avoided and a contribution made to developing an integrated understanding of the many neurophysiological, behavioral, and psychosocial factors which may be manifested in normality and psychopathology.

NEED FOR NEUROPSYCHOLOGICAL ASSESSMENT SERVICES

Among the many factors contributing to the development of this area of specialization within clinical child psychology, two stand out as particularly important. The first is related to the recognition that all handicapped children deserve a public education with as few restrictions as possible. The second factor is related to the increase in the number of children surviving potentially catastrophic trauma.

Prior to 1976, children suffering severe developmental disabilities including brain damage, cerebral palsy, developmental aphasia, mental retardation, and learning disabilities were inconsistently provided educational services. In 1976 the Education for All Handicapped Children Act was passed by Congress (Federal Register, 1976). Essentially, this act required all states to enact provisions such that handicapped children, no matter how severe their disability, could be provided with a public and nonrestrictive education.

The passage of this act brought national attention to the fact that a significant percentage of children suffered behavioral and learning disorders that were presumed to have a neurodevelopmental etiology. This was a rather large percentage of children, and some estimated the incidence of all handicapping conditions to range from 10% to 15% (Gaddes, 1981; Kirk, 1972; Mackie, 1969; Myklebust & Boshes, 1969; Rutter, Tizard, & Whitmore, 1970). For example, the incidence of only one neurologically based disorder of learning, dyslexia, is estimated to affect more children than the total number of children suffering cerebral palsy, convulsive disorders, and severe mental retardation (Duane, 1979). Thus, practically speaking, if one conservatively adopts a 12% incidence figure, out of 1,000 children 120 suffer from some behavioral or learning problem, the etiology of which is assumed to be due to anomalies in neurological development.

Assuming that these disorders could be differentiated clinically from similar but functional disorders, it was argued that neuropsychological assessment procedures should be used with children suspected of suffering a handicapping disorder (Gaddes, 1968, 1969; Rourke, 1975, 1976). Although not without criticism (e.g., Coles, 1978; Ross, 1976; Smith 1982), this perspective appears to be increasingly accepted, resulting in a need for more neuropsychological evaluation of behavioral and learning disorders.

Interacting with this increased need to differentiate functionally versus organically based behavioral or learning disorders is the recognition that the number of children surviving neurological trauma is increasing. On the basis of trends, one must expect that the number of neurologically handicapped children will increase significantly in the next decade.

Hynd and Willis (1988) present evidence that of the very low birth weight babies who survive due to technological advances in neonatal intensive care (Horwood, Boyle, Torrance, & Sinclair, 1982), approximately 64% require special education services by age 10 (Nickel, Bennett, & Lamson, 1982). Also, of the increasing number of children who are long-term survivors of childhood leukemia, a significant number seem to suffer serious learning and behavioral problems due to the treatment effects of intrathecal methotrexate and intracranial radiation (Elbert, Culbertson, Gerrity, Guthrie, & Bayles, 1985).

Finally, increasingly more children are surviving cerebral trauma. Bigler (1987) cites statistics that document that as many as three million persons a year may suffer from some form of head injury. Approximately 10% may be expected to suffer residual deficits of one kind or another. Since young adults and children form by far the largest population of those who suffer cerebral trauma, it is reasonable to anticipate a growing need for neuropsychological evaluations designed to serve these individuals. Consequently, as there is an increase in the number of children who suffer neurological and neuropsychological sequelae due to advances in medical treatment, so too will the need to assess the extent of neuropsychological development and the potential for intervention or rehabilitation.

PURPOSE OF NEUROPSYCHOLOGICAL ASSESSMENT

To comprehend fully what a neuropsychological evaluation entails, one must first have some knowledge of how the specialty of clinical neuropsychology is defined and how it differs conceptually from the traditional practice of clinical psychology. Although the distinctions provided here may be somewhat academic, they should be kept in mind in conceptualizing the purpose of neuropsychological assessment.

Lezak (1976) defined clinical neuropsychology as "an applied science concerned with the behavioral expression of brain dysfunction. It evolved in response to practical problems of assessment and rehabilitation of brain-damaged patients" (p. 3). Preferring the broader term, *human neuropsychology*, Hécaen and Albert (1978) suggested that the profession focuses on the study "of neural mechanisms underlying human behavior. This discipline is based on a systemic analysis of disturbances of behavior following alterations of normal activity by disease, damage or experimental modifications" (p. 1). Most writers would agree that neuropsychology is at the juncture of the neurological and behavioral sciences, with two distinct areas of specialization: adult neuropsychology and developmental neuropsychology.

The purpose of a neuropsychological evaluation of children would include: (1) differentiation of functional versus organic disorders; (2) differential diagnosis of subtypes of neurodevelopmental disorders; (3) differential diagnosis of assets and areas of deficit in children with organic disorders; (4) documentation of current neuropsychological status and, in patients with traumatic brain damage, estimation of the premorbid level of cognitive development; (5) assistance in the development of plans for rehabilitation and remediation; (6) documentation of the rate of improvement or deterioration; and (7) participation in research regarding the impact of altered neurological status on cognitive and behavioral development. Within this conceptualization, it would not be inconsistent for the clinical child psychologist to have either a minor or major role in actually providing treatment to the child or family.

Factors that make the neuropsychological assessment of a child uniquely different from that of a mature adult include: (1) the difficulty in judging the effects of brain damage on the developing organism; (2) the fact that children are more likely to have generalized brain damage whereas adults may have more focalized lesions; (3) the lack of adequate norms for many neuropsychological tests; (4) the general lack of research on children with neurological disorders; and (5) the often severe attentional problems one finds in children with neurological trauma that make lengthy assessment exceptionally difficult. Many other factors exist that make pediatric neuropsychological assessment uniquely different from that conducted with the adult (e.g., lack of a standard nosology for childhood neurodevelopmental and traumatic disorders). What should be kept in mind, however, is that the primary purpose of neuropsychological assessment with children is to document change in behavior and development due to alterations in the functioning of the central nervous system.

APPROACHES TO NEUROPSYCHOLOGICAL ASSESSMENT

As Chadwick and Rutter (1983) have noted, between 1940 and 1960 neuropsychological assessments were primarily concerned with answering the question as to whether or not signs of brain damage or organicity existed. Typical of the research during this period (and, unfortunately, today as well) are those studies that attempt to identify the best single test or item that distinguishes between brain-damaged and normal subjects. The focus of assessment has changed somewhat in the past couple of decades. The development of new technology (e.g., CT and MRI scans, brain electrical activity imaging techniques, measurement of regional cerebral blood flow) makes the use of psychological tests to localize brain damage less useful. The assessment of related behavioral deficits and subtle brain dysfunction is now more in demand. New questions demand new assessment practices and techniques.

Many new approaches and techniques have thus evolved over the past two decades, especially in terms of assessing the child patient. In addition to the more traditional batteries discussed at length in this volume, there is a variety of specialized neuropsychological assessment techniques (Benton, Hamsher, Varney, & Spreen, 1983; Spreen & Benton, 1977), diagnostic key approaches (e.g., Aaron, 1981), profile pattern techniques, predictive neuropsychological screening batteries (e.g., Satz, Taylor, Friel, & Fletcher, 1978), eclectic-development batteries (Taylor et al., 1984; Obrzut, 1981), and qualitative-clinical approaches based on Luria's theory (Christensen, 1979).

All of these approaches have value in conceptualizing different ways in which the neuropsychological assessment might best be conducted. However, the focus of the following assessment chapters will be on the two most popular batteries and an eclectic approach advocated by Hynd and Cohen (1983) and Obrzut (1981). This eclectic model is also consistent with that emphasizing a functional approach as discussed by Taylor et al. (1984).

Other approaches are not reviewed in this volume for several reasons. First, many of these approaches incorporate tasks included in the Halstead-Reitan batteries and are thus redundant. Second, those approaches that have potentially much to offer the clinician and researcher are as yet poorly validated through empirical research by independent investigators (e.g., Christensen, 1979; Benton et al., 1983). Finally, it is clear that the vast majority of clinicians receive their training in the procedures of neuropsychological assessment through workshop settings (Craig, 1979). Although perhaps deplorable (Satz & Fletcher, 1981) and at odds with formal training standards (Bieliauskas & Boll, 1984), few training programs exist in which formal education in pediatric neuropsychological assessment can be obtained. Furthermore, few internship experiences approved by the American Psychological Association (APA) offer appropriate training in pediatric neuropsychological assessment (McCaffrey, Malloy, & Brief, in press). Consequently, the evidence strongly indicates that the most widely used assessment procedures are learned in workshop settings where the focus is either on the Halstead-Reitan or Luria-Nebraska neuropsychological batteries. For these reasons, the neuropsychological assessment approach exemplified by the Halstead-Reitan and Luria-Nebraska batteries will be discussed at greater length. Although most of the available literature focuses on these approaches, the critical perspectives brought to bear on these procedures may, in all likelihood, be generalized to other neuropsychological assessment techniques and procedures. Prior to embarking on a discussion of the neurological and neuropsychological basis of behavior, some issues important to neuropsychological assessment with children and adolescents need to be addressed first.

ISSUES IN CLINICAL CHILD NEUROPSYCHOLOGY

There are many potential issues that could be discussed here. The two topics most relevant to the following chapters, however, are: What are the effects of brain damage in children and what is the neurological basis of learning disabilities? Other related issues, already covered in detail by Hynd and Willis (1988), are not discussed here. These include what constitutes appropriate preparation in the speciality of neuropsychology, what is the relationship between on-going neuropsychological development, cerebral insult and assessment practices, how does neuropsychological diagnosis interface with various diagnostic nosologies, and what is the relationship between psychometric "g," and neuropsychological functioning? For a discussion of the latter issues, the interested reader should refer to Hynd and Willis (1988).

Brain Damage in Children and Adolescents

The frequency and type of brain injury in children are important considerations. In one recent study, 62% of all new cases of head injury were cases under 24 years of age. Of these cases, about 50% were children under the age of 15 (Kalsbeek, McLauren, Harris, & Miller, 1980). In another study of 3,000 hospital admissions in the greater Boston area, it was found that 34% of the total number of head injuries occurred in children. Of this 34%, 26% had simple skull fractures, 18% had subdural hematomas, and 10% had depressed fractures (Schurr, 1979).

Basically, any head injury results in two kinds of injury. Primary injuries are those the brain receives directly because of the injury. Shearing of the parenchyma or vascular system, lacerations, or contusions are examples of primary effects. Secondary effects occur after a blow to the head and include anoxia, ischemia, and other metabolic derangements that can equally affect the recovery of neuropsychological functioning (Ward, 1985). Primary effects are often immediately observable while secondary effects may not be manifested until considerably later, even after recovery has begun.

Accidents and child abuse probably account for the vast majority of head injuries. Child abuse as a cause of brain injury is now receiving particular attention, probably because of an increased awareness of the effects of this type of injury, especially in the infant and young child (Friedman, Sandler, Hernandez, & Wolfe, 1981). The incidence of child abuse is striking. For example, Gelles (1978) found in studying 1,146 parents that 40% reported having pushed, grabbed, and shoved their children, 13% had hit them with an object, 3.2% had kicked, bitten, or hit them with their fist, and 1.3% had beaten them.

Neuropsychological testing as well as computed tomography (CT) or magnetic resonance imaging (MRI) may be useful in documenting the effects of child abuse as evidence exists that the jerking and shaking of the child's head may result in parieto-occipital shearing of tissue and veins (Rao & Kishore, 1984).

It is widely believed that, at birth, both cerebral hemispheres have the capacity to subserve most cognitive functions (Alajouanine & Lhermitte, 1965; Woods, 1980). Left hemisphere damage early in life would release the right hemisphere to develop language functions, for example. However, as the left hemisphere exerts more of a suppressive effect over time on the right hemisphere to subserve linguistic functions, this capacity of plasticity diminishes. Thus, according to Lenneberg (1967), by age five to seven the child's brain loses its capacity to become reorganized after significant brain damage.

Thus, one would expect, for example, results of brain damage in children older than five to resemble those found in an adult. In other words, the organization of the functional systems is well established and focal deficits will produce symptoms similar to those found in an adult.

Although a variety of factors may contribute to the recovery of function after a head trauma (e.g., diaschisis, neural regeneration, and neural sprouting), the most dramatic effect is cerebral reorganization. Evidence exists that if a very young child has a complete left hemispherectomy, language abilities may be reorganized and subserved by the remaining cortex in the right cerebral hemisphere (Milner, 1974). This phenomenon will also occur when the left hemisphere is significantly damaged early in development. Also, it appears that in these cases language has a priority, resulting in a significant depression of visual-spatial abilities. As Kolb and Whishaw (1980) have pointed out:

> The use of such words as plasticity and the emphasis placed on recovery of function in a great deal of basic research gives the impression that the brain has an unlimited potential for recovery and reorganization after injury . . . . The avilable evidence indicates that there are always residual and permanent deficits, and that extensive recovery is the exception, not the rule. (p. 422)

What can one conclude from this in terms of neuropsychological assessment? First, brain damage in children will result in general impairment across most domains assessed, perhaps because most trauma in children, compared to adults, is more generalized than focal (Kolb & Whishaw, 1980). Second, when focal damage occurs after the organizational pattern is reasonably well established (between five and seven years), the pattern of deficits on neuropsychological measures may resemble what one would expect with an adult (Boll & Barth, 1981). Third, since neuropsychological batteries currently available are based primarily on adult models of functioning, these batteries should probably be supplemented by additional assessment procedures in order to tap developmentally prominent functional systems (Satz & Fletcher, 1981). Fourth, when the mechanism of plasticity or cerebral reorganization occurs, significant neurological and neuropsychological deficits will most likely remain (Woods & Carey, 1979). Finally, there probably exist many secondary effects of brain damage, even when the injury itself is focal, that exert a significant effect on neuropsychological performance. It might well be for this reason that one often finds discordant results when comparing the effects of observable structural lesions on neuropsychological test results.

For instance, Von Monakov (1911) postulated that when damage occurs other parts of the nervous system, particularly the brain, are deprived of their normal stimulation. They therefore cease to function normally and represent distal effects of localized damage. Some support exists for this phenomenon, which Von Monakov termed diaschisis. Also, closed head injury can cause tearing and shearing of tissue that cannot be seen on CT or MRI scans. Behavioral effects may therefore result from an injury that cannot be documented through conventional neurological technology. In such cases, assessment by a psychologist may be most meaningful in documenting deficits. All in all, these considerations should reinforce the argument for the use of test results to clinically document the extent of impairment on neurological and cognitive processes and the evolution of recovery in relation to normal childhood development.

Learning Disabilities and
Neuropsychological Assessment

Kirk (1963) originally coined the term *learning disability* as being more acceptable than minimal brain dysfunction for describing the syndrome of normal ability in the presence of a severe inability to learn. Public pressure in the 1970s led to the passage of PL 94–142, in which learning disabilities (LD) were defined as a disorder in one or more of the basic psychological processes involved in understanding or in using language, spoken or written, which may manifest itself in an imperfect ability to listen, think, speak, read, write, spell, or do mathematical calculations. The term includes such conditions as perceptual handicaps, brain injury, minimal brain dysfunction, dyslexia, and developmental aphasia. (*Federal Register*, 1976, p. 46977)

The implication in this redefinition is, of course, that the disorder may "include" disorders known to have a neurological etiology. Inclusive criteria were later developed which generally required that (1) the child had at least average intellectual ability (IQ > 85); (2) that a discrepancy exist between measured intellectual ability and assessed academic performance in at least one area; and (3) that the child had not made academic progress despite conventional intervention (McCarthy, 1975).

A more recent attempt to refine the definition of LD suggested that "these disorders are intrinsic to the individual and *presumed to be due to central nervous system dysfunction*" (Hammill, Leigh, McNutt, & Larsen, 1981, p. 336; emphasis added). Although the field of LD has a rich history and owes its origin to those who were interested in subtle neurological disorders (Hynd & Cohen, 1983), concrete evidence of the presumed neurodevelopmental nature of LD was lacking. From cases of children who suffered learning problems similar to that found in brain-damaged adults, Morgan (1896), Hinshelwood (1895), and Bastian (1898) postulated that some developmental anomaly must exist in the region of the left angular gyrus. A series of reports by Hinshelwood (1900, 1902, 1909) reported more cases, and the neurological foundation of developmental LD was firmly established.

It has long been known that severe mental retardation is often associated with neurodevelopmental abnormalities (Crome, 1960; Freytag & Lindenberg, 1967; Jellinger, 1972; Malamud, 1964). These developmental anomalies have included many different kinds of dysplasias of the bulk growth of the brain (microcephaly, megalencephaly), dysplasias of the cerebral hemispheres (holoprosencephaly, agenesis), and dysplasias of the cerebral cortex (e.g., agyria, pachygyria, polymicrogyria).

In 1968 Drake provided the first autopsy evidence on a child with LD. He found an abnormal convolutional pattern in the parietal lobe (consistent with Bastian's 1898 hypothesis) and a thinned and stretched corpus callosum. These gross observations were of interest and correlated well with theory, but it remained for Galaburda and Kemper (1979) to provide the first clear-cut microscopic, histopathological study of a brain from a severely learning-disabled adult. Additional case reports by Galaburda, Sherman, Rosen, Aboitiz, and Geschwind (1985) have further documented that focal brain abnormalities may develop between the fifth-to-the-seventh month of gestation and that they may be related to severe learning problems. Hynd and Semrud-Clikeman (1988) provide a critical review of these and other such studies.

From a conceptual and clinical perspective these findings are important because they suggest that (1) the pattern of deficits would appear to disrupt those areas of the brain most involved in speech and language (see Chapter Two); (2) the pattern of deficits appears nearly random in the language areas and, if representative, suggests that each case of LD will represent a *unique* pattern of specific neurolinguistic deficits; and (3) there is no way any neuropsychological test battery can localize these anomalies. The most one might reasonably expect in terms of neuropsychological assessment is to project that, on the basis of test results, this person's pattern of deficits is consistent with that found in left hemispheric lesions affecting the parietal and temporal cortex.

Two additional points are important to note. First, subcortical structures such as the thalamus may also be involved (Galaburda & Eidelberg, 1982; Hynd & Semrud-Clikeman, 1988). Second, although no known etiology exists for these neurodevelopmental anomalies, there is some suggestion that they may result from chance variation, congenital factors, autoimmune disease (Rosen & Galaburda, 1984; Sherman, Galaburda, & Geschwind, in press) or, speculatively, cytomegalovirus (CMV) infection (Bray, Bale, Anderson, & Kern, 1981).

Thus, as these findings relate to neuropsychological assessment, it should be no surprise that LD children do fall between the neuropsychological profiles of normal and brain-damaged children (Selz & Reitan, 1979a, b). These findings also suggest why investigators such as Rourke and Finlayson (1978) find positive relationships between neuropsychological test performance and subtypes of learning disabilities. Finally, if these deficits are indeed typically localized to the left cerebral hemisphere, it should not seem inconsistent that LD children generally show impoverished verbal-linguistic skills when compared to performance abilities (Hynd, Obrzut, & Obrzut, 1981; Kaufman, 1979).

CONCLUSIONS

Based on the prior discussion, what can be concluded about the role and purpose of the neuropsychological assessment in the two populations most likely to be served by those conducting such evaluations? In working with the brain-damaged or learning-disabled child, the essential task facing the psychologist is to distinguish those behaviors that are believed normal in the child's social context from those that are maladaptive and due to alterations in the normal functioning of the central nervous system.

It is not inconsistent that severe behavioral deviancy due to neurological dysfunction can exist and be documented in a neuropsychological examination, but no positive findings may exist employing other sensitive neurodiagnostic tests or procedures. Indeed, deviations from normal patterns of behavior have historically been our most sensitive measure of neurological abnormality. The behavioral descriptions of developmental dyslexia proved accurate in distinguishing abnormal from normal neurological development long before postmortem studies were published. Similarly, behavioral differentiation of normality from mental retardation or schizophrenia preceded by centuries the documentation of neurodevelopmental abnormalities in the brains of many of those suffering severe or profound mental retardation or schizophrenia (Hynd & Willis, 1988).

An appreciation of the other neurodiagnostic procedures that are available and what they can contribute in diagnosis may help place the relative value of these procedures in proper perspective vis-à-vis the findings of neuropsychological assessment. For example, Figures 1.1 and 1.2 respectively show no lesion in a CT scan and a clearly documented lesion in an MRI scan. The behavioral effects of this tumor were dramatic and included seizures and diminished cognitive and neuropsychological functioning. The reason for the differences in documentation of the existence of the tumor relates to the technical parameters of these procedures. It is a reasonable expectation that the clinical child neuropsychologist should develop an understanding of what various neurodiagnostic procedures can and cannot reveal (Hynd & Willis, 1988).

All things considered, however, it is behavior that best reflects the integrity of our nervous system and for this reason it is the neuropsychological examination that most clearly defines which systems are normal from those that are dysfunctional. The neuropsychological

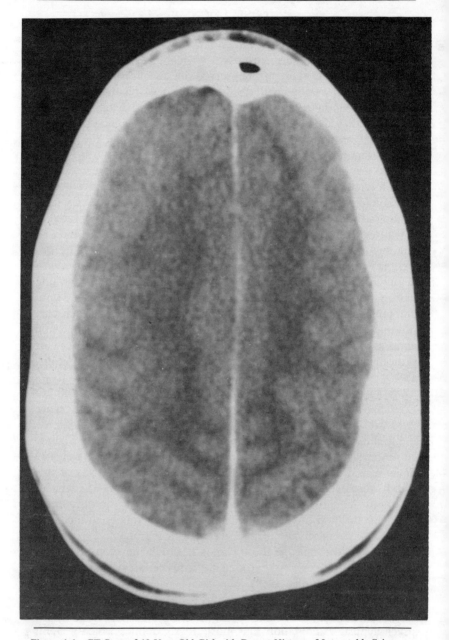

Figure 1.1 CT Scan of 10-Year-Old Girl with Recent History of Intractable Seizures.
This CT was read as normal.

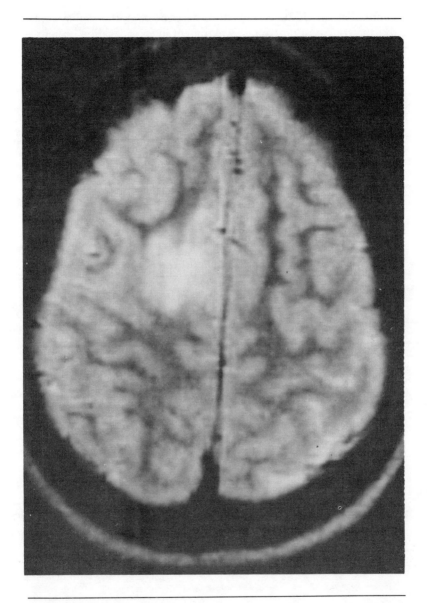

Figure 1.2   MRI Scan of Same Girl Depicted in Figure 1.1

This MRI scan shows an area of increased signal within the superior posterior
medial frontal area extending to the level of the corpus callosum. The pathology
report following surgical resection revealed a tumor consistent with the diagnosis of tuberous sclerosis (scans courtesy of M. Cohen).

examination should be employed to describe compromised systems, chart the course of on-going development in consideration of neuro-psychological dysfunction, and make predictions regarding long-term outcomes. To accomplish this requires an appreciation of neurology, the psychology of development and individual differences, and the psychometric procedures typically employed in neuropsychological assessment with children and adolescents.

2

BRAIN-BEHAVIOR RELATIONSHIPS: NEUROLOGY'S EARLY CONTRIBUTION

Localization of speech became a political question; the older conservative school, haunted by the bogey of phrenology, clung to the conception that the brain 'acted as a whole,' whilst the younger liberals and Republicans passionately favored the view that different functions were exercised by the various portions of the cerebral hemispheres.

—Head, 1926

To fully appreciate the complexities of human behavior, particularly of the developmental period, it is essential that one have some understanding of the central nervous system that allows for its expression. While many ideas have flourished with regard to the organization of the nervous system, it has only been since the early part of the nineteenth century that significant progress has been made in relating alterations in brain structure with observations regarding correlated behavior.

Recognizing that the developing understanding of how the brains of children are organized has been derived from the study of adults with known lesions, it becomes necessary to appreciate the historical evolution in thought regarding how the adult brain functions. For this reason, this chapter will provide an overview of some of the major historical developments in the past two centuries that have resulted in our present conceptualization of brain-behavior relationships. The contributions of psychology and current neuropsychological theory will be presented in Chapter Three. However, the historical context in which present conceptualizations of brain-behavior relationships may be viewed is provided here.

FUNCTIONAL LOCALIZATION

By the nineteenth century, neuroanatomists had identified the brain as the seat of cognition and had identified many of the major landmarks of the brain. The four lobes of the hemispheres had been identified, the reflex behaviors of the spinal cord were known, and the basic structure of the neuron had been described.

By the 1850s experimental and clinical investigations had progressed to the point where the function of the cortex was of major interest. Until the nineteenth century, the convolutions had been described as resembling the coils of the intestine, thereby suggesting that their arrangement had little functional significance. Then, at an accelerated pace, observations of patients' behavioral deficits were correlated to cortical pathology and cortical ablative experiments were conducted on animals. These investigative activities led to a more sophisticated level of appreciation for the arrangement and organization of the cerebral cortex.

Efforts to localize function on the cerebral cortex were hampered because of relatively crude techniques. Also, from a clinical perspective, there existed no widely agreed upon or standardized neurological or behavioral examination. For this reason, potentially important cases with well documented behaviors were often accompanied by exceptionally poor neuropathological descriptions. This was a considerable problem for those who attempted to construct models of cortical organization (Bastian, 1898).

Progress was made, however, in understanding the basic principles of cortical organization. Panizza (1785–1867), an Italian anatomist, demonstrated that the occipital cortex was important to vision in birds. Munk (1839–1912), a German, used ablation and found support for the idea that the retina projected to the visual or occipital cortex. Research with the localization of audition in the temporal lobes progressed more slowly, primarily because of the difficulty in assessing the effects of ablation in this sense modality in animals (Clarke & O'Malley, 1968). Figure 2.1 shows the major landmarks of the brain.

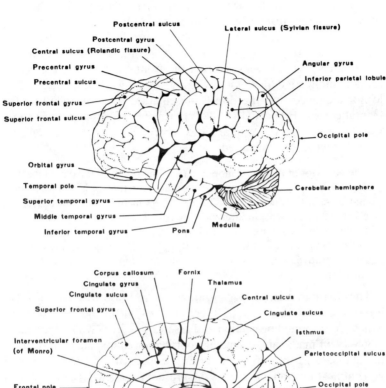

Figure 2.1   The Major Landmarks of the Human Brain.
Top: lateral view.   Bottom: medial view.

Localization of function in the frontal cortex was marked by controversy, however. By 1885, at least three theories had become popular. Based primarily on the work of Ferrier, one school of thought held that the frontal lobes controlled contralateral eye movements and facilitated attention. A second school, including the psychologist Wundt, believed that the frontal cortex was the center for all intellectual processes. Finally, there were those who, like Munk, believed that the dorsal musculature was controlled by the frontal cortex. Bianchi (1848–1927) probably represented best those who believed that the frontal lobes contributed greatly to intelligent behavior when he concluded:

> The behavior of mutilated monkeys (i.e., the removal of frontal lobes) displayed suppression of all manifestations of the spirit of initiative and of inquisitiveness . . . . This syndrome includes irrationale fear, errors of judgement, indifference towards things and living beings, a tendency to collect useless and filthy things (as do some idiots as well as the demented), and tics . . . all this phenomenology is sufficiently demonstrative of what I believe to be the function of the frontal lobes. (p. 232)

The neuroanatomical organization of the brain was also of great interest during this period. Flechsig (1847–1929) identified areas which were termed projection and association areas while Brodmann (1868–1918) made an outstanding contribution in mapping the patterns of cellular organization in the brain. In fact, Brodmann's work had gone almost unchallenged until the present decade. His contribution, as Bailey and Von Bonin (1951) stated, "has been accepted by physiologists as the divine authority and a vast superstructure has been built on this shakey foundation" (p. 192). Brodmann, of course, is best known for the identification of 52 cortical areas which are still referred to today.

A basic comprehension of the organization of the motor cortex was also developing. By the 1850s it was generally believed that the corpus striatum was responsible for motor movements. It seemed, at that time, that the motor cortex was not responsive to electrical stimulation. Technical problems were eventually overcome by Fritsch (1838–1891) and Hitzig (1838–1907) from Berlin who demonstrated that unilateral galvanic stimulation of the frontal lobe in unanesthetized dogs would evoke contralateral movements.

The cerebellum also came under study. Despite Gall's notion that sexual prowess was associated with the cerebellum (as reflected in a "bull neck"), work by Rolando (1773–1831) revealed that damage affected locomotion and motor strength. Apparently, Rolando's work was little known until Flourens (1794–1867) extended his studies. Using ablation, Flourens found that it was actually coordination, not locomotion or strength, that was primarily affected by cerebellar lesions. Other research revealed that vertigo and "oscillation of the eyes" could result from cerebellar damage, and Luciani (1840–1919) discovered that cerebellar lesions resulted in ipsilateral deficits. Thus, by the turn of the twentieth century it was well established that cerebellar lesions affected motor coordination and balance, and that lesions were manifested on the same side, or ipsilaterally.

LOCALIZATION OF SPEECH AND LANGUAGE

It was attempts to localize speech and language that provoked the most intense debate. To some extent the evidence has become more sophisticated in the past 100 years, but many of the issues remain unresolved today, particularly with regard to children. The models representing localization of speech and language so popular today may be more comprehensive and dynamic than those debated by Dejerine and Marie, for example, but they are based firmly on these early conceptualizations and underscore their historical importance. In this context, the ideas of Gall, Bouillaud, Broca, Jackson, and Wernicke are especially important.

Prior to discussing these individuals and their contributions, it should be noted that, as Benton and Joynt (1960) pointed out, there were ample case reports prior to 1800 describing patients with acquired aphasia. Of nine cases reviewed by Benton and Joynt, three had a non-fluent aphasia in which oral language was affected, accompanied by a right-sided paralysis; five of the other six had a fluent aphasia in which comprehension was affected. It should have been obvious to researchers even then that when an aphasia was accompanied by a paralysis, it always affected the right side. Benton (1984) suggests that one reason, perhaps, for not making this connection was the fact that those interested in aphasia during the eighteenth century were primarily interested in those aphasias presenting more dramatic symptoms (e.g., subtle linguistic problems or paraphasias) which were often not accompanied by motor involvement.

Initial efforts to localize speech and language focused on whether or not they were localized in the frontal lobes. Over time, the

controversy shifted to which convolution on the left side was involved and, with Wernicke's publication, what role the temporal and
parietal lobes had in language comprehension.

Franz Joseph Gall (1758–1828) was born in Baden and received his
medical training in France. After graduation he went to Vienna and
built a very successful practice. In 1791 he published his book,
*Medico-Philosophical Investigations of Nature and Art in Health and
Disease.* In this volume he scorned metaphysics and drew relevant
parallels between the behaviors of men and animals. He suggested
that various places in the brain had different functions. The emperor
in Vienna thought his writings were inappropriate for the prevailing
social climate and withdrew his permission for publication of the
book lest, as he humorously proposed, "some lose their heads over
it" (Schiller, 1970).

Gall's contributions to both psychology and medicine were many.
For instance, he suggested that the convolutions were the origins of
behavior and that the cranial nerves originated from the brain stem
rather than the two cerebral hemispheres. Also, he was one of the
first to note the symmetrical organization of the convolutions.
Relevant to this discussion, however, was Gall's observation that his
best and most intelligent students had protruding eyes, which suggested to him that the inferior frontal convolutions must be hyper-
developed (Schiller, 1970). He also studied two patients who had lost
the ability to recall words and attributed their deficits to lesions in
the frontal cortex.

At the age of 47, Gall went on a tour of Protestant Europe
lecturing about cerebral localization and how inferences could be
made by examining the skull. Actually, though, it was Spurzheim, his
colleague, who coined the term "phrenology" after he left Gall. Even
Gall disapproved of the term.

Luria (1980) has suggested that Gall's ideas regarding what
Spurzheim referred to as phrenology were not taken seriously by
those in scientific circles at that time. However, the popular press
and Spurzheim's sensational tour of America helped foster the perception that phrenology was an established scientific discipline. It
also had a profound impact on Horace Mann (1796–1859), widely
regarded as the father of American public education (Stone &
Schneider, 1965). He is reported to have suggested that "I look
upon phrenology as the guide to philosophy and the handmaid to

Christianity. Whoever disseminates true phrenology is a public benefactor" (quoted by Lahey & Ciminero, 1980, p. 14).

It is unfortunate that Gall's other more significant contributions have been eclipsed by his popularized views regarding phrenology. However, even in the latter he did make a contribution to the eventual successful efforts to localize expressive speech through his impact on Bouillaud.

Jean Baptiste Bouillaud (1796–1881), a disciple of Gall, was very interested in brain damage and its highly variable effect on humans. He argued that the association of focal brain damage with both profound and minor loss of motion and sensation was indicative of refined specialization.

Bouillaud also made some important observations with regard to speech. For example, he observed that when brain damage occurred, some related functions could be seriously affected while others might remain unaffected. The tongue, he observed, could be used quite successfully by an aphasic patient for eating but be severely affected when used for verbal expression (Heilman & Valenstein, 1979).

From his clinical observations, Bouillaud concluded that Gall was correct in his localization of speech in the frontal lobes but, like Gall, he observed no asymmetrical effect of lesions. This omission may be due, as Benton (1984) suggests, to his strong embracement of Gall's ideas concerning the bilateral frontal speech zones. It is of some interest that Bouillaud was so certain about the frontal lobe localization of speech that he offered 500 francs to anyone who could produce a patient with frontal lobe damage who was not also aphasic (Springer & Deutsch, 1981).

Bouillaud is important therefore in that he sustained Gall's notions that speech is a function of the anterior cortex. It remained for Broca, however, to provide the clinical evidence for localization of speech in the cortical regions.

Pierre Paul Broca (1824–1880) is, of course, given the credit for localizing speech in the left frontal cortex. His father was a former Napoleanic surgeon and Broca followed his example by traveling to Paris to study and practice medicine. He became a prolific researcher, publishing over 500 papers. He was one of the first physicians to experiment on the use of hypnotism during surgery and was an advocate of the emerging discipline of anthropology as a science (Goldstein, 1970).

In early 1861 Broca heard one of Bouillaud's students, Auburtin, make a presentation in which he discussed Bouillaud's notions about the frontal lobes and their role in speech. Broca, an adherent of faculty psychology, asked Auburtin to see one of his patients who had previously lost the ability to speak and write. The patient also had a right-sided hemiplegia and while he could comprehend some speech, the only word he could produce was "tan." Auburtin thought the patient demonstrated what Gall and Bouillaud had proposed.

When this patient died, Broca performed an autopsy which revealed a large cavity filled with fluid in the left hemisphere. When the fluid was drained it revealed a large lesion which involved the insula (later an important point for Marie, a critic of Broca's ideas), corpus striatum, the first temporal gyrus, and the second and third frontal convolutions.

Broca saw eight such patients and termed the language disturbance "aphemia." Trousseau, a critic of Broca's terminology, argued that the word "aphemia" was taken from a Greek work meaning "infamous" and thus had no relevance to what Broca was describing. Broca reportedly defended his choice of words but Trousseau's suggested term "aphasia" prevailed (Springer & Deutsch, 1981).

Later that same year, in 1861, Broca presented his data on his first patient to the Society of Anthropology in Paris. He concluded that the posterior part of the left third frontal convolution was important to speech. He termed it the "circonvolution du language" but Ferrier later referred to it as "Broca's convolution." On March 24, 1863, Broca's views were formally recorded by the Academie de Medicine.

Controversy immediately followed Broca's stated views. Weekly meetings and lengthy discussions took place and, two years later, Broca again presented his views, this time to the British Association for the Advancement of Science.

In relating his findings to those of the phrenologists, Broca (1863) suggested,

> In any case, it suffices to compare our observations with those that have preceded it [i.e., phrenologists'], to discard today the idea that the faculty of articulate speech resides in a fixed spot, circumscribed and situated under it-does-not-matter-which bump of the cranium, the lesions of aphemia have been found most frequently in the anterior part of the frontal lobe not far from the eyebrows and above the orbital roof; whereas in my patient they were much further back and much nearer to the coronal suture than the supraciliary ridge. This difference in location is incompatable with the system of bumps [phrenology] . . . . Here are eight instances in which the lesion was in

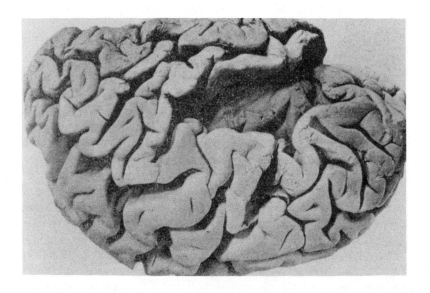

Figure 2.2 The Brain of Lelong, Who Was Broca's Second Case Study

Although the color and consistency of Lelong's brain was normal, it showed considerable atrophy. This 84-year-old sailor could not speak except for a few monosyllabic words (yes, no, and a few numbers) yet he seemed to possess adequate intelligence and verbal comprehension. Neither movement disorders nor paralysis were noted. Dejerine also examined Lelong's brain and agreed with Broca's description that the lesion was typical and involved the posterior third of the second and third frontal convolutions in the left hemisphere. Others, including Moutier, who examined Lelong's brain in 1908, thought it contained no lesion. (Quercy, 1943)

the posterior third of the third frontal convolution. This number seems to me to be sufficient to give strong presumptions. And the most remarkable thing is that in all patients the lesion was on the left side. I do not dare draw conclusions from this, I await new facts.

Interestingly, in 1906 Pierre Marie, a former intern of Broca's, sought out the brain Broca originally presented. He found, in addition to the lesion Broca described so carefully, a large parieto-temporal lesion as well (Bailey, 1970). The second brain described by Broca (see Figure 2.2) eventually also aroused some controversy (Quercy, 1943).

Broca was also interested in neurophysiological correlates of language lateralization and introduced the concept of hemispheric dominance, suggesting in 1865 that "most persons are naturally left-brained [gauchers du cerveau]" (cited by Henderson, 1986). Broca's contribution was immense and it set the stage for a further delineation of the circumscribed effects of brain lesions on speech and language disorders for a century to come.

John Hughlings Jackson (1835–1911) was born a farmer's son in Yorkshire, England. Despite his humble beginnings, he pursued a career in medicine and qualified at the age of 21. Deeply impressed with the writings of Carlyle and the associationist philosopher Spencer, Jackson at one time considered devoting his life to philosophy. The arguments of his father and Jonathan Hutchinson, a close friend and mentor, prevailed, however, and Jackson became one of the best known clinicians of that time (Greenblatt, 1965; Lennox, 1970).

In 1860 the National Hospital in Queen's Square opened in London and Jackson joined the staff in 1862. He worked there for 45 years during which time he published some 300 articles (Greenblatt, 1965).

Jackson is important for two reasons in the context of neuropsychology. First of all, he contributed greatly to a developing conceptual framework regarding the nature of seizures. For instance, in 1870 Jackson observed that a seizure might begin on the forehead, progressively involve the face, the arm and eventually the leg (it is today referred to as the "Jacksonian March"). It suggested to Jackson that the motor cortex in the brain must be somatotopically organized for this evolving seizure to occur (J. Taylor, 1956).

This was indeed an important deduction since, at that time, the precise role of the cortex was not clearly understood. In fact, it was the corpus striatum and thalamus that generated the most interest among those seeking to understand seizures. The cortex was viewed as important to mental functions, and perhaps, from the standpoint of Broca's observations, speech as well. Thus, in addition to acknowledging the important role of the cortex in seizures, it was Jackson's interest in the clinical nature of seizures that led him to investigate the role of the cortex in aphasia (Greenblatt, 1977).

Second, in terms of the popular notions of his day regarding the localization of speech, there is retrospective evidence that Jackson had differentiated between fluent and non-fluent aphasia prior to Broca's work (Greenblatt, 1977). Jackson observed the wide-ranging symptoms associated with aphasia and noted that a loss of articulate speech was almost always accompanied by a right hemiplegia. He concluded that the loss of speech was probably due to an obstruction of the middle cerebral artery and, since the paralysis was on the right side, that it must be due to some lesion in the left cerebral hemisphere. Thus, while Wernicke is usually given credit for distinguishing between fluent and non-fluent aphasia and providing the neuroanatomical evidence, it may well have been Jackson who was the first to differentiate the two disorders. Certainly, Jackson is highly regarded for his important contribution to clinical and behavioral neurology and his clinical-philosophical writings continue to generate interest (Critchley, 1986).

Carl Wernicke (1848–1904) was born to a civil servant from upper Silesia. He received his medical training in Breslau, where he returned after studying with Meynert in Vienna for six months. His enormously productive career was cut short by a fatal bicycle accident (Goldstein, 1970).

In contrast to Jackson, who was essentially a clinician, Wernicke began his career by studying anatomy with Meynert. Wernicke is best known for the publication at the age of 26 of his monograph *Der aphasische symptomenkomplex* (1874).

Based primarily on his experience as a clinician, Wernicke described sensory aphasia (also referred to as fluent aphasia) in great detail. He believed it was due to a lesion in the posterior aspects of the first temporal convolution in the left hemisphere. He acknowledged the existence of subcortical pathways connecting this region with that described by Broca some 11 years earlier. His excellent illustrations supported his arguments that the first temporal convolution was responsible for sound images while Broca's area was important for motor movement images. He also proposed, quite correctly, that if damage occurred to the fibers connecting these two regions a disconnection syndrome could result. Goldstein (1970) has suggested that it was the impact of Wernicke's illustrations that stimulated the publication of so many brain diagrams which remained popular for almost 50 years. Figure 2.3 shows the conceptual scheme of the central aphasias resulting from these efforts.

It is of historical interest that Wernicke was largely given credit for

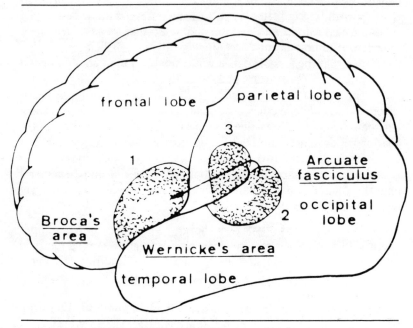

Figure 2.3   Lesion Sites in the Left Cerebral Hemisphere Associated with the Central Aphasias

A lesion in area 1 may result in Broca's aphasia (non-fluent), in area 2 in Wernicke's aphasia (fluent), and in area 3 a conduction aphasia wherein the ability to comprehend language (Wernicke's area) is disconnected from Broca's area, which is vital for expressive language. All three syndromes are characterized in part by deficits in repetition.

distinguishing between motor and sensory aphasia, when Jackson may have been the one to originally differentiate between the two. Perhaps because Jackson never published a widely circulated monograph and reportedly refused to even consider such a venture, lest "my enemies would find me out" (quoted by Lennox, 1970), Wernicke's monograph gained attention and thus firmly established him as the person who demonstrated the difference between various aphasia syndromes.

In fact, Wernicke's (1874) monograph was so provocative that Burkhardt (1891) decided to apply the ideas discussed by Wernicke to practice in the treatment of a psychotic woman. Her psychotic behaviors included manic agitation and verbigeration (continuous repetition of stereotypic words or phrases). Burkhardt believed that her agitation was a result of the dominance of the sensory speech zones over the motor speech zone. In a series of four separate operations he first disconnected Broca's area from Wernicke's, then resected the superior portions of the left temporal lobe, later removed portions of the cortex in the region of the angular gyrus, and finally removed what must have remained of the left hemisphere. Not too surprisingly, perhaps, the patient was no longer manic nor did she suffer verbigeration.

The evidence presented by Broca, Jackson, and Wernicke was not accepted without controversy. Bastian (1898), for example, suggested that the term aphasia be restricted to deficits of speech produced by lesions affecting only Broca's area. Bastian believed that a speech center was located in the right hemisphere and that sensory aphasia in particular really represented a form of amnesia. His conclusions were based largely on his critical reivew of case reports of patients with aphasia and word-blindness (dyslexia).

Pierre Marie, a vocal opponent of the ideas of Broca, argued that Wernicke's aphasia (sensory aphasia) was the only true type and that distinct forms of language disorders did not exist (Bailey, 1970). He believed that the variable symptoms seen in patients with language disturbances simply reflected associated intellectual impairments. He further suggested that Broca's aphasia was due to lesions affecting the area known by then as Wernicke's region (as Kussmaul suggested) and the speech disturbance or anarthria resulted from an encroachment of the lesion on an area he referred to as the quadrilateral space in the insular region.

Although controversy continued, the model of language organization developed then persisted and even today receives support in terms of its basic accuracy for the central aphasias. Further, while the evidence is not as great, it does seem that the brains of children are similarly organized for expressive and receptive functions (Hynd & Willis, 1988).

ORGANIC BASIS OF MENTAL DISORDERS

Even today, the theoretical issues associated with localization of speech and language hold center stage and engage the attention of a majority of researchers. Concurrent with the developments involving

Broca, Wernicke, and others who were interested in the localization of speech and language, important progress was also made in attributing deviant behavior to an organic etiology. It was reasoned that if functions such as limb movements and speech and language were localized in the brain, so too must other disorders be attributable to organic causes.

Thus, it was generally accepted by the early 1800s that mental disturbance was due to some disorder in the brain. The most popular notion at this time attributed psychosis to increased blood flow to the brain as a result of ambition and evil thoughts which, in turn, were associated with atheism and infidelity. As evidence in support of this notion, it was often pointed out that madness was uncommon in less developed countries where the expression of passion was more acceptable (Weinstein, 1984).

Therapy included efforts to equalize or balance blood flow to the brain through blood-letting, starvation, leeching, or by binding patients to keep them from reclining. Importantly, it was believed that a patient could be disturbed in one faculty while remaining rational in others. Thus, faculty-oriented therapy under this doctrine of moral insanity included efforts to re-educate or persuade the patient to change evil or unacceptable thoughts or behaviors.

The teachings of Gall, as popularized by Spurzheim, were particularly acceptable in this theoretical climate since they allowed for the localization of various faculties. The tenets of phrenology were enthusiastically embraced in the United States in the first half of the nineteenth century, spurred by Spurzheim's visit in 1832.

In fact, it was during this decade that the doctrine of moral insanity and the practice of phrenology first impacted on the American legal system. It served as the basis for the defense of a nine-year-old boy from New England named Major Mitchell, who had severely beaten and partially emasculated a boy one year younger than himself. This case was indeed a landmark since it was the first recorded attempt to absolve a defendant of admitted guilt due to his being assessed psychiatrically unfit to distinguish right from wrong. In support of the defense, Mighles stated:

> I am a believer in phrenology, as a science . . . . I have examined the prisoner's head—there is something remarkable in it—a very unusual depression. All heads are more or less deficient in symmetry, but the want of symmetry here, is quite remarkable. I have examined it repeatedly . . . and have come to the conclusion . . . that some injury

had probably happened to it. The right ear is lower than the left, and there is a considerable protuberance on that side . . . certain functions . . . of the brain may cease in consequence of a blow—the functional powers may be destroyed . . . while the rest continues undisturbed. Such is the doctrine of the books and I believe it. (Quoted by Walsh, 1985, p. 4)

Despite this authoritative testimony, Mitchell was found guilty and sentenced to nine years of hard labor. Thus, a potentially precedent setting case, in which the doctrine of moral insanity and phrenology would have been used to establish a foundation for the defense of diminished capacity, never came to fruition.

The case of Phineas Gage, as reported by Bigelow (1850), drew into question, however, some of Gall's notions. Gage was working with explosives and an accident occurred in which a 3½ foot rod was blasted through his left anterior cortex. Although Gage suffered behavioral difficulties as a result of his near fatal accident, speech was still intact. This case and others (e.g., Detmold, 1850) added fuel to the growing antilocalizationist movement, especially in the United States (Weinstein, 1984).

Yet even later in the nineteenth century, the use of phrenology as a foundation for a defense resting on the doctrine of insanity still found support. Perhaps the best example involved Edward Spitzka, who had long been interested in the neuroanatomical basis of insanity. He testified as to the congenital and acquired pathology that led to the insanity of Charles J. Guiteau, the man who assassinated President James Garfied. He testified that Guiteau not only had a positive family history for insanity but that it was reflected in an abnormal brain asymmetry. This, he testified, was reflected in a flattened right parietal lobe and a facial asymmetry characteristic of the insane. Unfortunately for Guiteau, he was declared sane and hanged. Spitzka continued his fight to prove Guiteau insane and was outraged when he was not allowed to view the autopsy. Writing in an editorial, Spitzka (1882) concluded regarding Guiteau's facial asymmetry:

Indeed photographs taken from different sides appear like photographs taken from different individuals. The right side is full of animation and . . . the left is dull and more vacant. It is the association of facial asymmetry, and crossed cranial asymmetry, with certain forms of hereditary and congenital insanity, that gives them their medico-legal importance. There is no more significant somatic anomaly in the insane than gross cranial deformity, for no other, aside from peripheral mal-development and the insane expression, points so directly to the organ which is the seat of healthy as well as of diseased mental action. (p. 388)

Through the efforts of those who focused on specific behavioral deficits that could be correlated to neurological pathology rather than attempting to relate global concepts such as insanity to neuropathology, the views of Gall and the doctrine of moral insanity gradually gave way. In addition to the continued documentation of the syndrome of aphasia (e.g., Brown-Sequard, 1877; Putnam, 1875), other behavioral syndromes including hemispatial neglect (Mitchell, Morehouse, & Keen, 1864) and word-blindness or developmental dyslexia (Bastian, 1898; Hinshelwood, 1900) were beginning to receive attention. Despite these advances, the notions of phrenology and contrasting evidence from experimental neurology were lending support to a rapidly developing wave of antilocalizationist sentiment.

DEVELOPMENT OF ANTILOCALIZATIONIST THOUGHT

Many different social, political and philosophical factors contributed to the rise and eventual prominence of antilocalizationist views. After World War I, the interest and support for science waned in Europe and the economic crisis resulting from the war brought social unrest and decreased financial support for empirical research. The prevailing Gestalt philosophy and rapidly developing dynamic psychology helped focus different approaches toward understanding human behavior and its deviations.

In neurology, the antilocalizationist philosophy was really an extension of the idea that the brain was a diffuse and interactive nerve network—a concept originated by Golgi (1843–1926). Golgi believed that the neurons in the brain formed an interactive net and, thus, any activity was likely to be generalized as opposed to specifically localized (Ferraro, 1970). Two individuals who are considered to be antilocalizationist are briefly considered in this discussion since each contributed uniquely to the notion of the multiplicity of functional localization in the cortex.

Constantin von Monakov (1853–1930) was born to the family of a Russian nobleman and, through a series of moves, eventually spent his formative years in Switzerland. Against his father's wishes he

decided to pursue a career as a physician. He was eventually ap-
pointed Professor Extraordinarius at the University of Zurich, where
he remained productive until his death at age 77 (Yakovlev, 1970).

von Monakov made a number of important contributions. Most
notable in the present discussion was his notion of chronogenic
localization. In this scheme, sequential processes, such as locomotion
or language, may have a locus for each segment of behavior but each
neural center is stimulated by and reverberates with other focal tracts
to produce a given behavior. Thus, function is the result of a historical evolution of neural activity. As von Monakov suggested in
referring to motor movements, ". . . in these the foci of the *Regio
Rolandi* undoubtedly play an important role. However, the significance or the meaning of an act is represented in the cortex in so
many multiple and manifold a way, that the local origin of its
elements can no longer be identified, it is simply common property
of the whole cortex" (von Monakov, 1914, p. 507).

As Riese (1950) pointed out, von Monakov may never have
received the attention his ideas fully deserved since his book, which
included some 1,033 pages and 3,174 references, was published at the
outbreak of World War I. It is significant, however, that the now
prevalent theories of Luria (1980) incorporate many of the early
notions developed by von Monakov. However, Lashley is probably
the best known proponent of an anti-connectionist theory of brain
organization.

Karl Spencer Lashley (1890–1958) was born in Virginia. He spent
his most productive years as a Professor at Harvard University.

Lashley is important because he combined the techniques of
psychology and learning with the ablative research paradigms of
experimental physiology. His research paradigms were quite crude,
however, in that he often failed to note what seemed to be important
differences in the way in which a goal was attained under different
ablations. He is widely known for his notion of the quasi-equivalence
of the two cerebral hemispheres. His views largely supported those
earlier propounded by Goltz in that he believed that the site of a
lesion was not as important as its size. He also believed that most of
the cortex played a vital role in memory and cognition. As Lashley
(1950) suggested:

> The equivalence of different regions of the cortex for retention of
> memories points to multiple representation. Somehow equivalent

traces are established throughout the functional area . . . . Briefly the characteristics of the nervous network are such that, when it is subject to any pattern of excitation, it may develop a pattern of activity, reduplicated throughout an entire functional area by spread of excitations, much as the surface of a liquid develops an interference pattern of spreading waves when it is disturbed at several points. This means that, within a functional area, the neurons must be sensitized to react in certain combination, perhaps in complex patterns of reverberatory circuits, reduplicated throughout the area. (pp. 478–479)

To anyone familiar with Luria's theory (1980), as discussed in the following chapter, it can be seen that his ideas of brain organization and the development of functional systems borrow significantly from earlier writers. This borrowing includes not only some of those investigators who attempted to localize function, but also von Monakov (1914), Lashley (1950), and other researchers not discussed here (e.g., Ukhtomskii, 1945)—all of whom viewed the brain as a complex network of interacting systems.

REAPPEARANCE OF EFFORTS
TO LOCALIZE FUNCTION

Many different factors have led to what has been termed a re-awakening of localizationist thought (Heilman & Valenstein, 1979). Some of the more important factors leading to this re-awakening are: (1) the realization that the findings of earlier clinical neurologists continued to be replicated in practice; (2) the fact that within the past 50 years new statistical procedures have been developed allowing researchers to determine which results of experiments are significant and which are not; (3) the development of behavioral paradigms (e.g., dichotic listening, tachistoscopic visual half-field paradigms, time-sharing procedures) which allow psychologists to assess neuropsychological processes more critically; and (4) the fact that neuroanatomical procedures have advanced so much that new mapping and imaging techniques provide a more articulate understanding of how the brain functions.

In addition to the above contributory factors proposed by Heilman and Valenstein (1979), other developments, equally important and often unacknowledged, deserve recognition. The economic depression that gripped the United States and Europe during the 1920s and 1930s followed by World War II, provided little incentive, let alone resource allocations, for the advancement of basic neuro-physiological research or associated technology. Considering the grim socio-economic conditions prevailing then, it is not surprising that scientific inquiry into the localization of function came to a standstill because researchers' conclusions reflected the pessimistic times. After World War II and with the launching of Sputnik in 1957, a series of public laws (e.g., National Defense Education Act, Elementary and Secondary Education Act) re-emphasized the importance of basic science research and provided funds for the improvement of basic education. Thus, with an increased commitment economically, basic science research could re-examine old ideas and develop new theories regarding brain-behavior relationships. And, with the advent of newly developed technology (e.g., CT scans) and clinical procedures (e.g., Wada technique), significant opportunities existed for correlating behavior with structural alterations due to disease or trauma.

Coupled with new technological advances came the realization that medical services, and in particular basic neuroscience research, could be more productive if it involved professionals representing a variety of disciplines including those trained in physics, statistics, nuclear engineering, computers, and psychology. With this broadened base came new perspectives and more fruitful research endeavors. Shortly after the middle of the century, the stage was set for a more productive inquiry into the localization of cortical and subcortical functions. Important in this regard was the contribution of psychology in understanding and documenting the nature, scope and development of individual differences.

3

PSYCHOLOGY'S CONTRIBUTION: EMERGENCE OF NEUROPSYCHOLOGY

There is a continuity of natural ability reaching from one knows not what height, and descending to one can hardly say what depth. I propose to range man according to their natural abilities . . . the method I shall employ . . . is an application of the very curious theoretical law of "deviation from an average."

—Galton, 1892

Since one of the primary roles of the neuropsychologist is to assess the changes in human behavior due to alterations in the functioning of the central nervous system (Craig, 1979; Hécaen & Albert, 1978; Lezak, 1976), some understanding of the historical antecedents of our current assessment and evaluation processes seems warranted. For example, while the neurologists of the last two centuries were attempting to understand neurophysiology, behavioral deficits and associated pathology, the developing discipline of psychology was attempting to document the neuropsychological basis for the range and deviations of human behavior and intellect.

BRAIN-BEHAVIOR THEORY: CONTEMPORARY DEVELOPMENTS

In terms of their impact on American clinical neuropsychology,

46

the work of Halstead, Reitan, Luria, and Geschwind are particularly important. The work of these individuals, and other more recent contributors, which has led to an understanding of brain-behavior relationships in children, will be discussed in the context of the theories they advanced. Their work is important because their theories cut across the life span of human development. It should also be pointed out that the contributions made by psychologists to the field of human neuropsychology is primarily due to advances in medical care which made possible the study of children and adults with head trauma, who would not have survived in centuries past. On the other hand, an understanding of the variability of normal human behavior enabled psychologists to assist those in the neurosciences in their attempts to comprehend the complexities of human behavior as they related to focal and diffuse brain trauma.

Ward Halstead, a physiological psychologist, began his work in the Division of Psychiatry and Department of Medicine at the University of Chicago in 1935. He was primarily interested in developing a theory regarding the nature of biological intelligence or the innate ability possessed by the individual. He differentiated this from psychometric intelligence which was reflected in most IQ tests. Using 13 measures he had narrowed down from his original 27 psychological and behavioral tests, Halstead collected data on 50 individuals and subjected them to a factorial analysis (Halstead, 1947).

Four factors emerged from his analysis which permitted the development of his theory. The C factor (integrative field factor) revealed to Halstead the individual's ability to adapt and integrate new information into his existing conceptual framework. The abstraction factor (labelled A) represented the individual's ability to extract essential features of some concept and discover its similarities or differences in relation to previously learned material. The P (or power) factor revealed the basic power or efficiency with which an individual's brain functioned. Finally, Halstead believed the directional factor (labelled D) represented the mode in which basic intelligence was reflected. This final factor was a weak one and one which Halstead found difficult to interpret.

Halstead is important because he was the first psychologist to use the techniques of measurement to construct a neurologically based model of cognitive function. Also, through his work with brain-damaged patients, he demonstrated that biological intelligence was severely affected by brain damage. Perhaps equally important as the contributions made by Halstead is the fact that one of his students not only carried on his work but improved upon the methods of clinical appraisal and extended the research to include children and adolescents.

Ralph Reitan's work continues today. He originally worked with Halstead in Chicago, then went to Indiana University Medical School where he refined Halstead's tests, conducted validating research of his own, and established himself as one of the best known neuropsychologists in the United States. Unlike Halstead, Reitan did not believe that biological intelligence is localized in the frontal cortex and demonstrated this in his own research (Reitan, 1964). Working in a neurosurgical unit, Reitan refined and eliminated some of Halstead's tests and developed some of his own which eventually resulted in the publication of the two batteries for children and an adult neuropsychological test battery. These tests and their related research are reviewed in detail in Chapter Four.

The importance of Reitan to American neuropsychology cannot be understated. He demonstrated theoretically and clinically that specially developed and well-validated tests can reliably discriminate brain-damaged patients from normals. He has also provided evidence of the executive function of the frontal cortex and established a solid foundation for future research efforts. Once this foundation was firmly established through the efforts of Halstead and Reitan, the writings of the Russian Luria made its impact on neuropsychology.

Alexander Romanovich Luria (1902–1977) initially trained as a psychologist and was captivated by the ideas of Freud's psychoanalytic theory. His early work focused on human emotions, cultural transitions due to massive collectivization of the agricultural economy in Russia, mental retardation, and psychological testing. He eventually completed medical school and spent most of World War II working in surgical wards with soldiers who suffered head wounds. Based on this experience, Luria developed the theory for which he is widely known today.

Pavlov's theory, the ideas advanced by von Monakov and Lashley, and the research of Vygotsky regarding higher cognitive processes provided the bases for the theories formulated by Luria. Basically, Luria (1980) believed that the brain could be conceptually and functionally organized into three units. This included the arousal unit (brain stem), sensory-input unit (temporal, parietal and occipital lobes), and the frontal cortex which was important in the planning and organization of behavior. Figure 3.1 depicts these three units. He introduced the concept of a functional system in which many different cortical zones might participate in producing any given behavior. The notion of pluripotentiality was also central to his theory in that any one cortical zone could participate in multiple functional systems. From the overview provided in the previous chapter, however, it can be seen that the ideas of functional systems and pluripotentiality were really not new but represented an integration of antilocalizationist theory (borrowed significantly from von Monakov and Lashley among others) with the tenets of cerebral localization. In this regard his theory obviously reflects neither a localizationist nor a mass actionist philosophy, since it incorporates notions common to both perspectives regarding brain-behavior relationships. As he remarked, ". . . we therefore suggest that *the material basis of the higher nervous processes is the brain as a whole* but that *the brain is a highly differentiated system whose parts are responsible for different aspects of the unified whole*" (Luria, 1980, pp. 32–33, italics original).

The importance of these highly interconnected units of the brain is vital in developing a theoretical and clinical perspective regarding brain-behavior relationships. The arousal unit provides cortical tone and participates significantly in attention-regulatory processes mediated in part by the frontal cortex and midbrain structures. While nearly a dozen theories exist as to the neurophysiological basis of the attention-deficit disorders in children (Zametkin & Rapoport, 1986), most of these theories implicate dysfunction in the arousal-frontal inhibitory system of the brain (e.g., Dykman, Ackerman, Clements, & Peters, 1971; Dykman, Ackerman, & McCray, 1980; Dykman, Ackerman, & Oglesby, 1979; Wender, 1974). The validity of this hypothesis was supported by a computerized tomography (CT) study in which regional cerebral blood flow (rCBF) was monitored during both on and off stimulant medication in children with attention deficits. Compared to normals, these children had a hypoactive frontal-inhibitory system off stimulant medication. When administered Ritalin, the metabolic activity in the regions associated with this arousal-regulatory unit increased to normal levels.

The second unit, or posterior cortical division, includes the temporal, occipital, and parietal cortex. The hierarchical organization

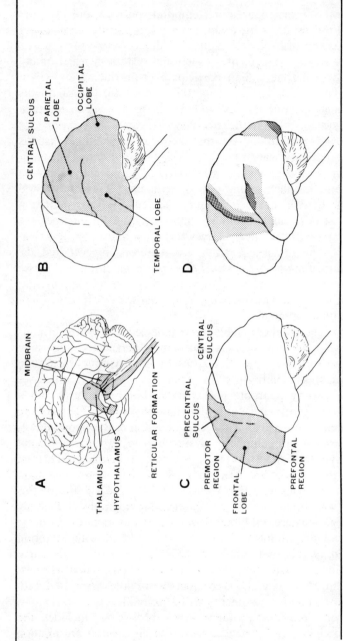

Figure 3.1 A: Luria's three functional units of the brain. B: Subcortical-arousal unit. C. Posterior cortical division or sensory input unit. D. Anterior cortical division or frontal regulatory unit.

Hierarchical organization of the cortical regions: Large dots—primary zones; medium-sized dots—secondary zones; small dots—tertiary cortical zones.

of these lobes includes the primary, secondary, and tertiary zones (see D in Figure 3.1). The primary zones are vital in sensory discrimination and perception. They have both afferent and efferent functions and lesions to these regions are typically associated with sensory-perceptual deficits (Luria, 1970).

The secondary zones in the posterior cortical region are believed important in sensory processing and in relaying sensory input from the primary zones to the tertiary cortex for more complex intermodal processing. The tertiary cortex is believed important in polymodal sensory integration such that sensory input may be processed cognitively and related to prior experience. Lesions to these regions often result in a marked disturbance of simultaneous synthesis of information (Luria, 1973, 1980).

The frontal, or anterior cortical, regions, once thought to be the seat of intelligence, are now known to be important in the maintenance of attention, setting of goal-directed behavior and in regulating sequential processes. As Luria (1973) suggested, the prefrontal regions "play a decisive role in the formation of intentions and programs, and in the regulation and verification of the most complex forms of human behavior" (p. 84).

While the evidence in favor of this conceptual model of brain-behavior relations seems well accepted, there are important developmental considerations that are particularly relevant to the appraisal of children with developmental disorders or those with known or suspected brain damage. With regard to normal neurological development, there is evidence that the process of myelination follows a predetermined sequence prenatally through, perhaps, adolescence or even adulthood (Campbell & Whitaker, 1986). For example, myelination of the motor and sensory system is generally completed by the age of six to twelve months. However, while the visual afferent system is typically fully myelinated by six to twelve months of age, the auditory system may not be fully myelinated until the preschool years. The cortical zones and their subcortical pathways (e.g., thalamic nuclei) continue to develop and myelinate during childhood with the corpus callosum, which interconnects the two hemispheres, fully maturing later in development, perhaps at age 10 or later.

Changes in neurodensity also occur and, similar to the process of myelination, considerable variability occurs across development with maturational changes being noted through 20 years of age. While changes do take place into early adulthood, it is believed that neuromaturational processes of the central nervous system are essentially 90% complete by the age of five to six years (Whitaker, 1981).

There is a presumption that as these cortical and subcortical regions (and hence sensory-cognitive systems) mature, a correlated evolution in observable behavior occurs. The early emergence of motor and somatosensory abilities thus seem to be correlated to the early maturation of the neural pathways associated with these systems (Hynd & Willis, 1988). Language abilities, however, are more slowly maturing behaviors and seem to be correlated to dynamic neuromaturational processes that continue through four to six years of age (Hynd & Willis, 1988; Whitaker, Bub, & Leventer, 1981; Willis & Widerstrom, 1986). Thus, with regard to the emerging behaviors observed in children, it seems a reasonable conclusion that as children mature an evolution may take place in brain-behavior relationships. In fact, Luria (1980) makes this point, indicating that with development, different discretely localized cortical zones may interact to produce a given behavior.

> The structural variation of the higher mental functions at different stages of ontogenetic (and, in some cases, functional) development means that their cortical organization likewise does not remain unchanged and that at different stages of development they are carried out by different constellations of cortical zones . . . thus . . . the character of the cortical intercentral relationships does not remain the same at different stages of development of a function and the effects of a lesion of a particular part of the brain will differ at different stages of functional development. (Luria, 1980, pp. 34–35)

While most of Luria's work focused on adults with known brain lesions and his evidence in favor of his formulations was primarily of a qualitative, clinical nature, his contribution to present conceptualizations of brain-behavior relations was immense. As an exceptional clinician, Luria left not only his important theoretical ideas but also a clinical and qualitative approach to assessment. This approach was in direct opposition to the techniques developed by Reitan (Luria & Majovski, 1977) and will be discussed in more detail in another chapter.

Norman Geschwind (1926–1984) was a neurologist whose contribution to neuropsychology was cut short at the height of his career. Geschwind excelled early in his career. Graduating from Harvard

Medical School and after an internship in Boston, he completed a fellowship at the National Hospital in London and returned to Boston in 1955.

As a neurologist, Geschwind was interested in the behavioral effects of alterations, both traumatic and experimental, in the functioning of the central nervous system. His contributions in this context are many. He was an early advocate of the subspecialty in neurology of behavioral neurology (Damasio, 1984). In particular, he was vitally interested in disconnection syndromes, neuroanatomical asymmetries and their relation to language, handedness and neurodevelopmental factors related to cerebral dominance and dyslexia (Damasio & Galaburda, 1985). As a behavioral neurologist, he paved the way for renewed efforts to understand the interrelationships between neuronal growth and differentiation and subtle deficits in behavior and learning as found in patients with developmental dyslexia.

Based on his work documenting the normal human brain, in which 65% have a larger left planum temporale (posterior aspect of the superior temporal lobe) and only 11% a larger right one (Geschwind & Levitsky, 1968), numerous investigators sought to document natural asymmetries in brains, many of which are believed to be vital in speech and language (Kopp, Michel, Carrier, Biron, & Duvillard, 1977; Rubens, Mahuwold, & Hutton, 1976; Teszner, Tzavaras, Gruner, & Hécaen, 1972; Wada, Clarke, & Hamm, 1975; Witelson & Pallie, 1973). The asymmetry favoring the left language areas has been the most extensively studied and, although few in number, the autopsy studies of the brains of those with developmental dyslexia suggest an increased incidence of brain symmetry (Galaburda, Sherman, Rosen, Aboitiz, & Geschwind, 1985). Hynd and Semrud-Clikeman (1988) provide a critical review of these studies.

The importance of these studies, which were directly stimulated by work of Geschwind, lies in the fact that they provide the only concrete source of data to suggest that children with developmental learning disorders, such as dyslexia, may suffer from brain abnormalities related to disturbances in neuronal migration during the fifth to seventh month of gestation. While there are definite methodological problems associated with these studies (Hynd & Semrud-Clikeman, 1988), they are of considerable theoretical importance.

Geschwind and Behan (1982) and Geschwind and Galaburda (1985a, b, c) have also proposed some interesting neurodevelopmental relationships between deviations in normal patterns of brain asymmetry (as found in the postmortem studies of dyslexics), handedness, and increased incidence of auto-immune disease. While these ideas have generated some controversy (Satz & Soper, 1986) and may raise more questions than answers about brain behavior relationships in children (Hynd & Semrud-Clikeman, 1988), they have encouraged research into relationships that might otherwise have been poorly examined.

The work of others is also important in the context of the neuropsychology of children. Kinsbourne (1970), for example, has provided a model of hemispheric attention that helps place perceptual and linguistic asymmetries in a developmental cortex (Hynd & Willis, 1988). Satz (1976) has contributed greatly in terms of stimulating research into developmental issues regarding cerebral dominance (Satz & Strauss, 1986), the effects of aphasia in children (Satz & Bullard-Bates, 1981), and in proposing a model of handedness that provides a more theoretically sound model explaining left handedness (Satz, Orsini, Saslow, & Henry, 1985). Coupled with unique and important contributions from many other researchers (e.g., Hécaen, 1956; Kimura, 1961; Lenneberg, 1967; Penfield & Roberts, 1959; Sperry, 1964; Zangwill, 1960), the stage was set for the emergence of neuropsychology as a distinct discipline.

EMERGENCE OF NEUROPSYCHOLOGY

Referred to as simply "the symposium" and much later as the International Neuropsychological Society (INS), Henry Hécaen, the French neurologist, established in 1949 the first international effort to bring together multidisciplinary researchers to discuss the brain and behavior (Zangwill, 1984). Variously held in Salzburg, Lake Constance, Paris, and later in Cambridge, England, the purpose was to informally bring together researchers from psychology, psychiatry, and neurology. Eventually, the INS grew to include a conference held in the United States and one in Europe on an annual basis. To further facilitate communication among these researchers, Hécaen in 1956 first proposed the idea of establishing an international journal devoted to neuropsychology (Zangwill, 1984).

Under Hécaen's leadership, *Neuropsychologia* has flourished since its first publication in 1963, with the avowed purpose of bringing together in one journal human and animal research on brain-behavior relationships. Over the past two decades it has published nearly 1,500 articles, of which nearly 20% have reported research on animals (Ettlinger, 1984).

Since the journal *Cortex* was first published in 1964, a number of different professional journals in clinical, developmental, and experimental neuropsychology have appeared. Also, in recognition of the needs of clinicians in neuropsychology, the National Academy of Neuropsychologists (NAN) was formed in the early 1980s. Division 40 (Clinical Neuropsychology) of the American Psychological Association was also formed and the American Board of Professional Psychology (ABPP), and the American Board of Clinical Neuropsychology awarded diplomates in Clinical Neuropsychology. Thus, through the efforts of theorists and clinicians, such as Halstead, neuropsychology in the mid-1980s became a well-established discipline incorporating research techniques and theory from clinical and experimental neurology as well as physiological, experimental, and clinical psychology.

The clinical application of the quantitative approach in differentiating pathological from normal variability due to alterations in the functioning of the central nervous system has become a service offered by an increasing number of applied psychologists. In order to meet the growing demand for such clinical services, particularly for children, several approaches to clinical child assessment have evolved over the past two decades. The next chapter examines the Halstead-Reitan approach which, over the last 20 years, has gained a significant degree of acceptance as the standard in clinical practice. While its popularity has perhaps waned in recent years with the publication of the Luria-Nebraska Battery—Children's Revision and the increasing use of eclectic approaches (Obrzut, 1981; Taylor, Fletcher, & Satz, 1984), the Halstead-Reitan approach is still widely employed in both clinical and research settings.

4

HALSTEAD-REITAN BATTERIES FOR CHILDREN

The frontal lobes, long regarded as silent areas, are the portion of the
brain most essential to biological intelligence. They are the organs of
civilization—the basis of man's despair and of his hope for the future.
—Halstead, 1947

It will be recalled from the previous chapter that Halstead (1947,
1951) distinguished between what he termed biological intelligence
and psychometric intelligence. Biological intelligence for Halstead
was that capacity with which an individual is innately endowed
whereas the latter is that revealed by intelligence tests. Although he
recognized that these two broad factors were related, his work focused
on identifying the components of biological intelligence.

Using the tests that contributed to the four factors noted earlier
(Chapter 3), Halstead developed the Halstead Impairment Index
and validated its use on patients with documented brain damage. It
was found that patients with frontal lobe injury did six times as
poorly on the Impairment Index as did normal controls, and three
times as poorly as controls with damage to other areas of the brain.

In a historical context, Halstead's conclusions regarding the importance of the frontal cortex mirrored the beliefs of earlier theorists
including Gall, Wundt, Hitzig, and Bianchi (Hynd & Willis, 1985).
Reitan, a student of Halstead, further developed Halstead's test
battery through a careful empirical evaluation of the discriminant
validity of the tests employed. Although some have claimed that
Reitan's contributions are atheoretical (e.g., Luria & Majovski,
1977), it is now clear that Reitan not only refined Halstead's test
battery and made it clinically useful, but also provided evidence that

intelligence was not a function of the frontal lobes. In general, Reitan's (1955) work confirmed that the frontal lobes contribute more to the organization and execution of behavior than they do to intelligence. Clearly, though, his major contribution has been in further developing and validating tests for clinical neuropsychological assessment (Reitan, 1955; 1966; Reitan & Davison, 1974).

According to Reitan (1980), a neuropsychological test battery must be designed to meet three criteria: (1) it must be comprehensive, assessing the full range of human capabilities; (2) it must be sensitive both to global neurological impairment and to focal deficits; and (3) it must demonstrate technical adequacy and provide results useful in clinical evaluation.

Using these criteria, Reitan and his colleagues developed two batteries for use with children. For children between the ages of nine and fourteen the Halstead Neuropsychological Test Battery for Children is used. This battery contains seven of the original Halstead tests and other measures developed or modified by Reitan. The Reitan-Indiana Neuropsychological Test Battery is for children between five and eight years of age. This battery is primarily a downward extension of the older children's battery, although six tests were specifically developed for children of this age (Selz, 1981). Table 4.1 provides an overview of the measures employed in each battery. It should be noted that the appropriate Wechsler intelligence test (WPPSI, WISC—R) and the Wide Range Achievement Test—Revised (WRAT—R) are also administered as part of these batteries. Appendix A provides a chronology of many of the studies examining the psychometric and clinical utility of these batteries.

FINDINGS WITH BRAIN-DAMAGED CHILDREN

Typical of the approach characterized by Chadwick and Rutter (1983), Reed, Reitan, and Kløve (1965) evaluated the ability of these tests to discriminate between 50 brain-damaged and 50 age-matched normal children. It should be noted that in nearly all these studies positive neurological damage had to be verified through neurological exam, history, and positive electrophysiological findings (e.g., slowing, spikes). Paired T-tests on 27 variables (Wechsler-Bellevue and the neuropsychological tests) revealed that the brain-damaged children performed significantly less well on all variables. Of some theoretical interest is the fact that the brain-damaged children did

TABLE 4.1

Halstead-Reitan Neuropsychological Test Batteries for Children and Adolescents[a]

Test Battery	Age Range	Subtests and Scales	Abilities Assessed
Reitan-Indiana Neuropsychological Test Battery for Children[b]	5–8 years	Category Test[c]	Complex concept formation, basic reasoning abilities, intelligence
		Tactile Performance Test	Right/left-sided sensory perception, sensory recognition, spatial memory
		Finger Oscillation Test (Finger Tapping)	Right/left-sided motor speed
		Sensory-Perceptual Measures	Sensory localization, sensory perception, sensory recognition
		Aphasia Screening Test	Letter identification, follow directions regarding right/left hands, copy simple geometric shapes, compute simple arithmetic problems
		Grip Strength Test (Dynamometer)	Right/left-sided muscle strength
		Lateral Dominance Examination	Assesses right/left-sided preferences
		Color Form Test	Cognitive flexibility, sequential reasoning
		Progressive Figures Test	Visual-spatial reasoning, cognitive flexibility, sequential reasoning
		Matching Pictures Test	Perceptual generalization, ability to categorize
		Target Test	Pattern perception, ability to attend to and copy visual-spatial configurations
		Individual Performance Test	Visual perception, visual-motor integration
		Marching Test	Visual-motor integration, coordination

(*Continued*)

TABLE 4.1 Continued

Halstead Neuropsycho- logical Test Battery for Children	9–14 years	Category Test	Complex concept formation, basic reasoning abilities, intelligence
		Tactual Performance Test	Right/left-sided sensory perception, sensory recog- nition, spatial memory, manual dexterity
		Seashore Rhythm Test	Sustained auditory attention, perceive and match different auditory rhythmic sequences
		Speech Sounds Perception Test	Sustained attention, auditory perception, auditory-visual integration
		Finger Oscillation (Finger Tapping)	Right/left-sided motor speed
		Tactile, Auditory, and Visual Imper- ception Test	Perceive unilateral and bilateral simultaneous sensory stimulation
		Tactile Finger Recognition Test	Ability to perceive and localize sensory stimulation
		Finger-Tip Number Writing Perception Test	Ability to report numbers written on the finger tips
		Tactile Form Recognition Test	Sensory recognition, tactile-visual integration
		Aphasia Screening Test	Letter identification, follow directions regarding right/left hands, copy simple geometric shapes, compute simple arithmetic problems
		Grip Strength Test (Dynamometer)	Right/left-sided muscle strength
		Trail-Making Test	Conceptual set shifting, memory attention (A and B)
		Lateral Dominance Examination	Right/left-sided preference

(Continued)

TABLE 4.1 Continued

---

[a] For a more detailed overview of these batteries the reader is referred to Reitan (1974), and Selz (1981). Table adapted from Hynd and Snow (1985) with permission.

[b] The Reitan-Indiana is normally administered along with the Wide Range Achievement Test—Revised (WRAT—R) and the WPPSI or WISC—R (depending on the child's age). The Halstead Test Battery is normally administered along with the WRAT and WISC—R. Depending on the child, the neuropsychological evaluation with these two batteries may take between four hours to all day to complete.

[c] It will be noted that many of the subtests on the Reitan-Indiana and Halstead battery are the same, but have been modified for younger children. Performance on these measures is evaluated according to the child's level of performance (normative), pattern of performance, right/left-sided differences, and whether or not pathognomonic signs are present. Selz (1981) provides diagnostic procedures for identifying learning-disabled and brain-damaged children using these tests.

---

most poorly on linguistic tasks, suggesting initially that brain damage in children results in problems different from those in adults. Boll (1974) replicated and extended this study and found similar results.

Focusing on the older children's battery, Boll and Reitan (1972a, b, c) conducted a series of studies in which the performance of brain-damaged and matched (race, gender, and age) normal children was examined. These studies revealed several important results. First, similar to the earlier studies, the brain-damaged children generally did less well on all the intellectual (Wechsler-Bellevue) as well as neuropsychological measures (Boll & Reitan, 1972b). Second, the vast majority of the measures autocorrelated, especially for the brain-damaged patients (Boll & Reitan, 1972a). Third, there was greater correlation between scores on the neuropsychological measures for the brain-damaged children than for the normals with measures of general cognitive ability (IQ scores).

In evaluating these early findings it must be pointed out that in no study did the number of brain-damaged subjects exceed 50. Thus, the magnitude of these findings is of considerable interest since the reliability of correlations based on such small samples is usually poor. Also, it should be noted that in a series of earlier investigations Reitan (1971a, b) found similar results in an examination of the performance of brain-damaged and normal children on specific tests in his battery.

With regard to the younger children's battery, Reitan (1974) compared 29 brain-damaged children ($\bar{X}$ CA = 7.0) with 29 normal children matched for gender and age. In this study, the Wechsler

Intelligence Scale for Children (WISC) was used along with the WRAT and the entire Reitan-Indiana Neuropsychological Test Battery. Significant differences between the normals and brain-damaged children were found on all but one of the 41 measures employed. Only Grip Strength (dominant hand) failed to distinguish between the two groups. Of considerable interest, of the 41 variables employed in the analysis, the WISC Full Scale IQ discriminated between the two groups better than any other single variable. In fact, of the nine most sensitive tasks, eight were WISC variables. Similar to other studies (Boll, 1974; Reed, Reitan, & Kløve, 1965), it was found that brain damage to the young child has severe consequences in language development and nearly comparable effects on per-ceptual-performance abilities. This is in contrast, of course, to the evidence (often controversial) that in the mature adult generalized brain damage results in greater impairment of perceptual-motor abilities than verbal-conceptual abilities (e.g., Ernhart, Graham, Eichman, Marshall, & Thurston, 1963). Some more recent evidence with children indicates the pattern of Performance < Verbal IQ, as found in adults, may also hold true for children (Dunleavy, Hansen, & Baade, 1981).

These studies strongly suggested that children with generalized brain damage perform less well than normals on measures of intelligence and other neuropsychological tests. However, it remained for more recent investigators to provide evidence regarding the ability of these measures to localize cerebral dysfunction. Good preliminary evidence existed with adults suggesting that lateralized neurological trauma resulted in predictable effects on verbal and performance IQ as well as on other measures of neuropsychological functioning (e.g., Fields & Whitmyre, 1969; Kløve, 1974; Parsons, Vega, & Burn, 1969).

However, Camfield et al. (1984), in one of the few recent studies to address this issue in children, evaluated neuropsychological test performance in children with right or left hemisphere pathology. Their subjects included 13 left and 14 right temporal lobe epilepsy patients. The means of localization was consistent unilateral EEG findings. As the age ranged from six through seventeen, portions of the Halstead-Reitan or Reitan-Indiana were used in addition to the WISC—R or WAIS, WRAT, and the Personality Inventory for Children (PIC). Basically, in the group of 27 unilateral temporal lobe patients no significant behavioral or cognitive differences existed between those with the right versus left focal lesions. Most children scored normally on the neuropsychological measures. The only significant finding was that 10 of the children were identified as maladjusted on the PIC.

Although these results are not consistent with some previous studies (e.g., Fedio & Mirsky, 1969; Stores, 1978; Stores & Hart, 1976), they do provide a point for discussion. First, unlike previous investigators, these authors chose to limit their pool of subjects by not including those whose IQs were in the mildly mentally retarded range. Also, they excluded patients who had other significant lateralizing neurological findings (e.g., hemiparesis). Finally, they excluded patients with perisylvian foci (Lombroso, 1967). Their negative results were perhaps due to these exclusionary criteria. The employment of these criteria served not only to restrict the range of intellectual impairment possibly related to left- or right-sided pathology but also biased the potential findings toward those patients with more inferior temporal lobe pathology. Given such a bias, there may have been some tendency to select patients with pathology affecting the limbic structures and not the semantic-linguistic abilities associated with the left perisylvian region. Although speculative, perhaps it is this factor that contributed to the findings of emotional-behavioral maladjustment in so many of the subjects. Also, although it was noted that the majority of the patients suffered partial-complex seizures, no report was given on whether the seizures were due to brain-damage injury or were ideopathic in nature. Finally, the majority of the patients had less than one seizure per year (17/27).

The point in discussing this study is that it typifies the many potential conceptual and practical problems that exist in attempting to document the localized effects of neuropsychological impairment, particularly in children who tend to suffer generalized brain damage, compared to adults who are more likely to suffer focal damage (Kolb & Whishaw, 1980).

Although some evidence exists suggesting that, as in adults, left or right focal damage in children results in linguistic or spatial deficits respectively (e.g., Fedio & Mirsky, 1969; Stores, 1978), perhaps an equally important question is: What effect does brain damage exert on developing cognitive abilities? Several studies have addressed this important point using the Halstead-Reitan Battery. Basically, it appears that cerebral damage acquired early in development (after perhaps age three) may have a profound effect on the acquisition of new learning (Reed, Reitan, & Kløve, 1965; Reitan, 1974; Selz,

1981). As children develop and acquire normal cognitive abilities, the effects of brain damage later in adolescence or early adulthood are usually less severe and are related often to adaptive and problem-solving skills.

Prior to examining the literature regarding the use of these batteries with learning-disabled children, the factorial validity of the Halstead-Reitan Battery warrants a brief comment. Relatively few studies have examined the factorial validity of these batteries, perhaps because of the difficulty in finding sufficient numbers of brain-damaged subjects and the length of time it takes to administer a complete neuropsychological examination to a child. The results of the few studies that have been conducted (e.g., Crockett, Klonoff, & Bjerring, 1969; Daugherty & Moran, 1982) are difficult to interpret since different measures were included: Some studies focused on normals (Crockett et al., 1969) and others employed patients with questionable neurological impairment and a small sample size (Daugherty & Moran, 1982). The study by Crockett et al. (1969) is one of the best on the Reitan-Indiana Battery. On testing 240 normal children and using a principal component analysis with varimax rotation, these researchers found that at least nine different factors existed. Those factors accounting for the most variance included: (1) a perceptual-analytic factor (15.5%), (2) a motor-speed factor (8.3%), and (3) a verbal-concept formation factor (6.9%). One may wonder why verbal or performance scale IQ scores did not contribute significantly to the factor findings. They did not because Crockett et al. did not include IQ scores in the analysis; instead, only the Wechsler subtests were included. As might be expected, considering the positive relationship between intelligence measures and neuro-psychological tests, the Block Design and Vocabulary subtests did load significantly on the first and third factors respectively. In fact, the Wechsler Vocabulary Subtest performance contributed the most of all 28 variables to Factor III, while the Block Design and Object Assembly subtests contributed the most of all the variables to Factor I. Similar results might be expected with large samples of generalized brain-damaged children.

FINDINGS WITH LEARNING-DISABLED CHILDREN

Because of legislation passed by the 94th Congress (PL 94–142) regarding the required provision of free, appropriate, and nonrestrictive educational services to children and adolescents with severe learning disabilities, many studies have examined the ability of these batteries and tests to discriminate between normal, learning-disabled, and brain-damaged children. Of course, the presumption is that these children (and those previously labeled as minimally brain damaged or MBD) suffer neurological deficits of some sort that place them conceptually somewhere between normality and confirmed brain damage. A more recent definition, adopted by a number of professional organizations representing those who serve the learning disabled, suggests that learning disabilities "are intrinsic to the individual and presumed to be due to central nervous system dysfunction" (Hammill, Leigh, McNutt, & Larsen, 1981, p. 340). This definition continues to suggest that hard evidence of organicity (e.g., hemiparesis, aphasia, damage documented by computed tomography) is not a requirement for such a diagnosis but that CNS dysfunction must be the suspected cause.

Controversy has raged for several decades about these conditions and, as Benton (1974) suggested over a decade ago, this area of investigation "is truly a mare's nest" (p. 50). Benton's conclusion was indeed kind since it had been previously suggested by Gomez (1967) that one should equate "minimal cerebral dysfunction" with "maximal neurologic confusion." Concerns and controversy continue (Hynd & Willis, 1988; Gaddes, 1985) with respect to these concepts, but some progress has been made in providing concrete evidence of the neurological basis of these disorders (e.g., Drake, 1968; Galaburda & Kemper, 1979; Hynd, Hynd, Sullivan, & Kingsbury, 1987; Lou, Henriksen, & Bruhn, 1984).

One of the first comprehensive studies to employ a complete battery of academic, cognitive, and neuropsychological tasks was conducted by Doehring (1968). He compared 39 boys between the ages of 10 and 14 years who were significantly delayed in reading but who otherwise appeared normal. Of the 103 measures employed, he found the normals to be superior on 62 of the measures. When two neuropsychologists gave blind ratings of the subjects as having either "no cerebral dysfunction" or "definite cerebral dysfunction," their correct classification rate was statistically significant. The conclusion, of course, is that this study provided evidence for the neuropsychological basis of severe learning disabilities.

Reitan and Boll (1973) reported a much more comprehensive and revealing study, however. They examined brain-damaged, control, and two groups of children with minimal brain dysfunction. These latter two groups included 25 who showed primarily academic deficiencies but who did not manifest behavioral problems, and another group of 19 who exhibited primarily behavioral problems. The 94 children in these four groups were administered the Wechsler Intelligence Scale for Children (WISC), Reitan-Indiana Neuropsychological Test Battery, Wide Range Achievement Test (WRAT), and other relevant neuropsychological tests.

Analysis of the data generated by Reitan and Boll (1973) revealed a strong group effect, no main effect for sex, and evidence that some of the measures distinguished well between groups. There appeared to be a general ordering of the subject groups, with the control group performing best overall and the brain-damaged children performing poorest across nearly all domains. The MBD groups (academic difficulties & behavior disordered) seemed to perform in the range between the extremes provided by the control and brain-damaged children. These data add fuel to the argument that learning-disabled children perform as though they suffered "minimal" brain damage or dysfunction since their profile appears to fall between normality and documented neurological pathology.

Of interest, and the reason for devoting so much attention to this study, is the fact that it is the cognitive measure (WISC) that best separates or distinguishes between all the groups. In fact, insofar as can be determined from the data reported, it is *only* verbal IQ that significantly distinguishes between all the possible group pairwise comparisons. In other words, it appears that cognitive measures, particularly Verbal IQ, best distinguish between groups of children presumably representing a distribution of neurological integrity.

It could be argued that the children simply did less well on tests of cognition and neuropsychological ability because of the attentional deficiencies frequently found in children with CNS dysfunction. Thus, from this perspective the deficits on measures of neurological integrity may not reflect impaired neurological processes but rather impaired attention, which cuts across all domains of performance. From a neurological perspective this argument represents a case of misattribution whereby behavior might be thought to encompass arousal, attention, ability, and so on. In this case these factors are conceptualized as representing *discrete* components of behavior, which may interact but are nonetheless separate. Thus, arousal or attention may independently or synergystically affect ability or performance on a task. From a neurological perspective these components of behavior are seen as more *interactive*. Consequently, it would be conceptually consistent that children or adults with minimal or overt brain damge would do poorly across most domains wherein the components of attention (e.g., arousal, focusing, sustaining) are all impaired. In fact, deficits in attention are one of the most frequently cited problems in children with behavioral disorders (e.g., attention-deficit disorder, dyslexia), and neurological evidence exists concerning the pathology of various regions of the cortex involved in these children (Duffy, Denckla, Bartels, & Sandini, 1980; Galaburda & Kemper, 1979; Hynd & Hynd, 1984; Lou, Henriksen, & Bruhn, 1984). In all the studies cited here the pathological group (brain-damaged, LD, behaviorally disordered) consistently performed less well and variably across most of the domains assessed. This may be the reason why the "hit rates" reported in many studies appear to be so high. For example, on the basis of an earlier study by Reitan and Boll (1973), Selz (1977) attempted to articulate the neuropsychological profile of normal, learning-disabled and brain-damaged children on the Halstead-Reitan Battery. Using 13 measures (including the three WISC IQ scores), she was able to classify in a discriminant analysis 80% of the subjects correctly. The classification errors consisted of classifying subjects as less impaired than their original group membership suggested (Selz & Reitan, 1979a).

As a component of the 1977 study, Selz had Reitan blindly classify subjects into the three groups based on his examination of the neuropsychological test results. He achieved an 81% hit rate. In a final study, Selz and Reitan (1979b) developed a set of classification rules based on the regression equation for use with clinical populations. Not surprisingly, the normals did the best, the learning-disabled performed second best, and the brain-damaged did the least well. It may well be that brain damage (to any degree) affects attention or basic neurological processes related to cognition (IQ) and attention (e.g., memory) and it is for this reason we see this ordering of groups: normals, LD, and BD. Table 4.2 provides the scaled scores for the Selz and Reitan (1979b) classification rules system. After the battery has been administered and scored, the scaled scores for each measure are determined and summed. The group cut-off scores that resulted in the fewest misclassifications are as follows: < 19 = normal; 20–35 = learning disabled; > 36 = brain damaged. Selz (1981) elaborates this system.

TABLE 4.2
Scaled Scores for Rules System

Test	Score			
	0	1	2	3
Level of Performance				
1. Category—errors	≤34	35–55	56–74	75+
2. Tactual Performance Test				
(TPT)—Time (in min)	≤6	6–9.9	10–13.9	14+
3. TPT—Memory	6, 5	4	3	2, 1, 0
4. TPT—Localization	3+	2	1	0
5. Trails A—time (in sec)	≤15	16–25	26–35	36+
6. Trails B—time (in sec)	≤39	40–55	56–70	71+
7. Speech—errors	≤10	11–15	16–20	21+
8. Rhythm—correct	25+	21–24	16–20	≤15
9. Verbal IQ	90+	80–89	70–79	≤69
10. Performance IQ	90+	80–89	70–79	≤69
11. Full Scale IQ	90+	80–89	70–79	≤69
12. Tapping, preferred				
hand—no. of taps	34+	30–33	26–29	≤25
13. Tapping, nonpreferred				
hand—no. of taps	30+	27–29	23–26	≤22
Pattern				
14. Pattern IQ[a]	≤.99	1.00–1.40	1.41–1.75	1.76+
Right-left differences				
15. Tapping[b]	.04−.16	.03 to −.15 .17−.30	−.16 to −.25 .31−.40	≤−.26 .41+
16. Grip[b]	.0−.20	−.01 to −.06 .21−.26	−.07 to −.12 .27−.32	≤−.13 .33+
17. TPT[b]	.11−.49	.10 to −.05 .50−.65	−.06 to .20 .66−.80	≤−.21 .81+
18. Name writing—preferred hand (converted score— see Table 4.3)[b]	10, 8	6, 4	2	0
19. Name writing-difference (converted score—see Table 4.3)[b]	6	4	2	1
20. Tactile Finger Recognition: Right hand errors— left hand errors[b]	0, 1	2	3	4+
21. Finger-tip Number Writing: Right hand errors— left hand errors[b]	0–2	3–4	5–6	7+

(Continued)

TABLE 4.2 Continued

Pathognomonic signs

22. Imperception—errors[c]	0	1	2	3+
23. Tactile Finger Recognition—errors[c]	0–3	4–5	6–8	9+
24. Finger-tip Number Writing—errors[c]	0–7	8–10	11–14	15+
25. Tactile Form Recognition—errors[c]	0	1	2	3+

Aphasia battery	Score for deviant performance
26. Constructional dyspraxia	2
27. Dysnomia	3
28. Spelling dyspraxia	1
29. Dysgraphia	2
30. Dyslexia	2
31. Central dysarthria	2
32. Dyscalculia	2
33. Right-left confusion	1
34. Auditory verbal dysgnosia	3
35. Visual number dysgnosia	3
36. Visual letter dysgnosia	3
37. Body dysgnosia	3

From *"Rules for Neuropsychological Diagnosis: Classification of Brain Function in Older Children"* by M. Selz and R.M. Reitan, *Journal of Consulting and Clinical Psychology*, 1979, *47*, 258–264. Copyright 1979 by the American Psychological Association. Reprinted by permission.

[a] Pattern: Extreme scatter on the subtest scores on the Wechsler scale is abnormal. The following conversion measures the degree of scatter: (largest subscale score— smallest subscale score) ÷ mean of subscale scores.

[b] Right-left differences: The following tests compare performance of the right and left hands. Ratios for 15–17 are derived from this formula: 1− (nonpreferred hand ÷ preferred hand). The scores in 18 and 19 are derived from the conversion formulas presented in Table 4.3.

[c] Pathognomonic signs: For these tests, normal performance consists of perfect performance. Allowance was made for the fact that even normal children tend to make more errors than adults.

In another series of studies, Rourke and his colleagues, using primarily multivariate procedures, have identified specific patterns of neuropsychological test performance among subtypes of LD

TABLE 4.3
Name Writing Test Conversions

Preferred Hand		Nonpreferred Hand		Difference between Hands	
Time (sec)	Converted Score	Time (sec)	Converted Score	Time (sec)	Converted Score
				—ᵃ	2
0–9	10	0–29	7	0–4	4
10–14	8	30–69	6	5–9	10
15–19	6	60–69	4	10–14	8
20–24	4	70–84	2	15–19	6
25–50	2	≥85	1	20–24	4
≥50	0			25–44	2
				≥45	1

From "Rules for Neuropsychological Diagnosis: Classification of Brain Function in Older Children" by M. Selz and R. M. Reitan, *Journal of Consulting and Clinical Psychology*, 1979, *47*, 258-264. © Copyright 1979 by the American Psychological Association. Reprinted by permission.

Note: If subject cannot write name with either hand, classify as brain damaged. Each subject receives three scores: the lower the score, the poorer the performance.

ᵃ Preferred hand is slower.

children (Rourke & Finlayson, 1975, 1978; Rourke & Gates, 1981; Rourke & Telegdy, 1971). Overall, these results strongly suggest two conclusions. First, the performance of LD children is distinctly different on neuropsychological tests employed on the Reitan-Indiana and Halstead-Reitan Batteries from the performance of normal and brain-damaged children. It appears that LD children, as a group, have relatively poorer verbal-expressive skills compared to performance abilities, right-left orientation difficulties, and attentional-memory deficits (Obrzut, Hynd, & Obrzut, 1983; Rourke & Finlayson, 1978; Teeter, 1983). Second, and an important point conceptually as well as clinically, LD children with distinctly different neuropsychological profiles turn in quantitatively different performances on measures of academic achievement (e.g., Rourke & Gates, 1981). For instance, Rourke and Finlayson (1978) found children with severe deficits in math to have well-developed auditory-verbal skills but poorly developed visual-spatial skills. Complex psychomotor and tactile-perceptual tasks were also a problem for these children. A less disabled group of math-deficient children primarily had problems in reading and spelling. Thus, if attentional deficits by ability inter-actions do occur as suggested, performance may be differentially affected. In this regard it appears that the neuropsychological examination using the Halstead-Reitan and Reitan-Indiana Batteries can provide meaningful data in the differential diagnosis of subtypes of LD.

However, it must be recognized that these batteries do not ade-quately assess more in-depth neurolinguistic processes frequently impaired in children with subtle language disorders. Supplemental tests are probably needed for this aspect.

CONCLUSIONS

Research of well over two decades suggests that the tests employed on the Halstead-Reitan and Reitan-Indiana Batteries are reasonably successful in differentiating the normal, brain-damaged, and learning-disabled child. Generally, the brain-damaged child performs signi-ficantly below the level achieved by the LD child, who, in turn, performs below the level of the normal child. Performance on tests of intelligence seem to contribute very significantly to the differen-tiation between these three groups of subjects. Most of the measures employed in these two batteries discriminate to some degree be-tween normal and brain-damaged children. Some limited evidence exists for using the performance on these batteries to localize focal lesions. However, considerably more research is needed with groups of focally impaired children before any definitive statement can be made in this regard. Finally, it must be concluded that although these batteries may be useful in discriminating between normality, brain damage, and learning disability, to use them in any other capacity clinically (e.g., localization of dysfunction, prediction of recovery rates) probably steps beyond the bounds of what is supported by the available literature.

5

THE LURIA-NEBRASKA NEUROPSYCHOLOGICAL BATTERY— CHILDREN'S REVISION

With the spread of Luria's ideas and theories to other areas of psychology, the need for a children's test battery based on Luria's theories has become evident . . . the Luria-Nebraska Battery, as well as other instruments based on this neuropsychological theory, will significantly alter the practice of child assessment during the next two decades.
—Golden, 1981

The theoretical orientation provided by Luria (1980) has indeed had a significant effect on how many neuropsychologists both conceptualize and assess brain-behavior relations in adults and children. Based on the theory outlined in Chapter 3, Luria advocated a hypothesis testing approach to clinical assessment which focused on a qualitative interpretation of a patient's performance on some given task considered reliable in assessing a component of an involved functional system.

Such a qualitative approach relies heavily on the clinical skill of the psychologist who, through experience, must have some knowledge as to what constitutes normative behavior. With children, however, Golden (1981) pointed out that neurologically based behaviors evolve over the course of development and, thus, there was a need for developing a test battery for children based on Luria's (1980) theory but scored in a quantitative fashion with the scores derived from normative data. From this orientation, the Luria-Nebraska Neuropsychological Battery—Children's Revision (LNNB—CR) was developed to assess neuropsychological functioning in children eight to twelve years of age. The theory and formulation of this battery is discussed by Golden (1981).

Development of the battery centered around revision of the adult version of the test, the Luria-Nebraska Neuropsychological Battery (LNNB; Golden, Hammeke, & Purisch, 1978). The process of revision involved administration of the LNNB to a group of children with above-average achievement to identify inappropriate items and instructions which might need modification in order to be more appropriate for children. Three versions of the battery were tested with groups of normal children until a fourth and final form was completed. This version was then administered to a normative group of 125 normal children, 25 at each age level. Performance norms were then calculated for each age level (by year) and item scores derived from these data.

The battery consists of 11 scales and a total of 149 items. The scales of the LNNB—CR are: Motor Functions, Rhythm, Tactile, Visual Functions, Receptive Speech, Expressive Speech, Writing, Reading, Arithmetical Skill, Memory, and Intellectual Processes. Table 5.1 summarizes abilities associated with each scale. Each item within the battery is scored on a 3-point system. A score of *0* equals performance less than one standard deviation below the mean, a score of *1* equals performance between one and two standard deviations below the mean, and a score of *2* equals performance greater than two standard deviations below the mean. Item scores are summed within each scale, and this total is then converted to a T-score which has a mean of 50 and a standard deviation of 10.

CRITICAL PERSPECTIVES

Before a review of the research on the LNNB—CR, development of the battery must be considered further. Golden (1981) argued that the LNNB—CR was formulated based on a developmental-neuro-psychological model. Utilizing basic principles from Luria's theory (1973, 1980), Golden outlined five general stages of development. The first four stages involve development of the cortical arousal mechanisms, the primary and secondary motor areas, and the sensory primary, secondary, and tertiary zones (see Luria, 1980). These stages are said to be completed by the time a child reaches eight years of age (Golden, 1981). The fifth stage concerns the

TABLE 5.1

Luria–Nebraska Neuropsychological Battery—Children's Revision (LNNB—CR)

Scales	Abilities Assessed
1. Motor Skills	Motor speed, coordination, ability to imitate motor movements
2. Rhythm	Perceive and repeat rhythmic patterns, sing a song from memory
3. Tactile	Finger localization, arm localization, 2-point discrimination, movement discrimination, shape discrimination, stereognosis
4. Visual	Visual recognition, visual discrimination
5. Receptive Speech	Follow simple commands, comprehend verbal directions, decode phonemes
6. Expressive Language	Ability to read and repeat words and simple sentences, name objects from description, use automated speech
7. Writing	Analyze letter sequences, spell, write from dictation
8. Reading	Letter and word recognition, sentence and paragraph reading, nonsense syllable reading
9. Arithmetic	Simple arithmetical abilities, number writing and number recognition
10. Memory	Verbal and nonverbal memory
11. Intelligence	Vocabulary development, verbal reasoning, picture comprehension, social reasoning, deductive reasoning

Table adapted from Hynd and Snow (1985) with permission.

development and maturation of the tertiary zones of the frontal lobes which, Golden believes, does not commence until adolescence. Therefore, in constructing a neuropsychological test appropriate for children eight to twelve years of age, it was necessary to exclude those items designed to measure prefrontal lobe skills since, according to the developmental model, these areas are not yet developed and fully functional with children of this age. Golden states that this was the approach (i.e., the selection and elimination of items based on neuropsychological development) used in formulating the LNNB—CR.

There are, however, two major problems with this argument. First, Golden presents little or no supportive data for these five stages of development. Some limited data have since been published (McKay et al., 1985). The primary concern here is Golden's contention that the prefrontal lobe areas do not mature until adolescence. He did not cite any empirical evidence in support of his notions, and, in fact, an examination of Luria's 1973 book (which served as a major guideline for the battery) indicates that Luria believed that the prefrontal lobes mature at about ages four to seven. Interestingly, recent research conducted by Passler, Isaac, and Hynd (1985) suggests that the development of behaviors associated with the frontal lobes in normal children occurs in a stepwise, multistage fashion. Some behaviors are fully developed by age six to seven and others are not mastered until age twelve or older. Even more recent research confirms these findings and points to potentially important gender and racial effects on tasks that are presumed to assess frontal lobe functions (Becker, Isaac, & Hynd, 1988). Thus, the exclusion of items that may assess executive functions, perhaps regulated in part by the frontal lobes, does not seem to be justified by available research.

The second problem centers around the extent to which the construction of the battery actually reflects an adherence to a developmental model. Golden (1981) argues that there were two guiding viewpoints which could have been utilized in constructing a children's test version. The guiding principle of one perspective is the notion that children are merely less skilled adults and, therefore, adult versions of tests are simply made easier. In his opinion, the two tests which characterize this approach are the WISC—R and the Halstead-Reitan Children's Batteries. The second approach considers developmental sequences which, as stated earlier, supposedly guided the construction of the LNNB—CR. However, it is difficult to perceive that developmental aspects were really considered with the item selection for the battery. As discussed earlier, the construction of the LNNB—CR involved the administration of the adult version to a group of children with above-average achievement in order to identify inappropriate items and instructions which may have needed modification. How did this reflect item selection based on a developmental model? More specifically, if one wants to follow Golden's model, how is it known that these criteria eliminate only those activities that are contingent on prefrontal lobe skills? For that matter, why were only children with above-average achievement utilized? Theoretically, would not children with average abilities also miss items relying on prefrontal lobe skills? In general, it appears that the development of the LNNB—CR more closely approximates the first viewpoint (i.e., that children are less skilled than adults and therefore tests should simply be made easier) since item selection was apparently based merely on a group of above-average children's abilities to successfully complete items from the adult version of the test. In essence, the criteria do not appear to reflect developmental considerations to any great extent.

At this point, and with these concerns in mind, it is important to consider the research that has been completed with the LNNB—CR. Most of the studies have focused on the use of this battery with brain-damaged and normal subjects or with learning-disabled children. The interested reader will find a chronology of many of the published research studies involving the LNNB—CR in Appendix B.

FINDINGS WITH BRAIN-DAMAGED CHILDREN

A primary means of validating neuropsychological assessment procedures is to examine the ability of the test(s) to discriminate between brain-damaged and non-brain-damaged groups. Several studies have addressed this issue with the LNNB—CR (Carr, 1983; Gustavson, Golden, Wilkening, Hermann, Plaisted, MacInnes, & Leark, 1984; Sawicki, Leark, Golden, & Karras, 1984; Wilkening, Golden, MacInnes, Plaisted, & Hermann, 1981). Wilkening et al. (1981) used a sample of 76 brain-damaged (diagnosed on the basis of neurological exam and supporting evidence, e.g., CT scans) and 125 normal controls. Each was administered the LNNB—CR, and a statistically significant score was found between the two groups. Univariate F tests with each of the 11 scales were all significant. Most importantly, a discriminant analysis was also computed which yielded an accuracy hit rate of 91.3% for the normal controls, 65.3% accuracy rate for the brain-damaged children, and an overall accuracy rate of 81.59%. Additionally, Wilkening and his colleagues examined the effectiveness of a criterion analysis system for differentiating the subjects. The criterion system involved comparison of the child's T-scores on each of the 11 scales to the value yielded by the following regression formula: $82.02 - (.14 \times \text{Age in Months})$. Using the system of more than two T-scores above the value yielded by the regression formula as indicative of brain-damaged performance,

Wilkening et al. (1981) found accuracy hit rates of 80% for the normals, 69.7% for the brain-damaged children, and an overall accuracy of 86.2%.

The design and results of the study by Gustavson et al. (1984) are very similar to those of the Wilkening et al. report. In the validation part of this study the authors used a sample of 91 normal controls and 58 brain-damaged children. Statistical tests indicated a significant difference between the groups. Follow-up tests were significant for all 11 scales. The regression formula criterion was also examined in this study. The criterion of more than two scores above the regression formula value yielded correct classification rates of 98% for the normals, 65% for the brain-damaged children, and an overall classification rate of 85%. The criterion of at least two scores above the regression formula value yielded correct classification rates of 89% for the normal, 79% for the brain-damaged, and an overall classification of 85%. And the criterion of one or more scores above the regression value yielded a classification rate of 66% for the normals, 95% for the brain-damaged children, and an overall rate of 77%.

A within-scales factor analytic study has also been completed with the LNNB—CR (Gustavson, Wilkening, Herman, & Plaisted, 1982). The sample used in this study consisted of 201 children—76 brain-damaged and 125 normal. Each subject was administered the LNNB—CR, and the scales of the battery, using the items as variables, were factor analyzed. The number of factors found ranged from one to nine. Plaisted, Gustavson, Wilkening, and Golden (1983) argued that using factor analysis in this way allowed for identification of the basic neuropsychological processes which comprise the higher cortical functional systems. However, Stambrook (1983) commented on methodological problems with respect to this technique with the LNNB, problems that also appear applicable to the results with the LNNB—CR. These problems are the difficulty in using factor analysis with variables that are assessed on ordinal scales which have few categories (Comrey, 1978) and the fact that different groups (i.e., brain-damaged and normals) were included in the analysis without noting that the factor structures of these groups may differ (Spiers, 1982). Given these methodological difficulties, Stambrook concludes that the data generated by the within-scales factor analysis cannot be considered in terms of construct validity (which is often assessed using factor analysis) for the scales of the battery.

The issue of construct validity of the Luria-Nebraska batteries is important and warrants further discussion. Satz and Fletcher (1981) have pointed out that the major criterion used to demonstrate construct validity of the LNNB has been determining the effectiveness of a subtest in discriminating between brain-damaged and non-brain-damaged groups. The literature suggests that this is also a primary criterion with the LNNB—CR. However, this type of evidence alone does not yield much information on what constructs the test battery is assessing. In general, the issue of the lack of construct validity information with the LNNB and the LNNB—CR with brain-damaged and normals continues to be a concern (Snow & Hynd, 1985a).

Some data are available, however, on the concurrent validity of the LNNB—CR with brain-damaged and normal children (Berg, Bolter, Ch'ien, Williams, Lancaster, & Cummins, 1984; Tramontana, Klee, & Boyd, 1984; Tramontana, Sherrets, & Wolf, 1983). Tramontana et al. (1983) compared the LNNB—CR with the Halstead-Reitan. The sample comprised 22 hospitalized child and adolescent patients. Each subject received both the LNNB—CR and the Halstead-Reitan and scores for the batteries were intercorrelated. The results indicated that 193 of the 374 coefficients were significant. Correlations between the 11 scales of the LNNB—CR with the Halstead-Reitan sum of scaled scores ranged from .54 to .80. The authors felt that, in general, the pattern of correlations among the variables tended to support the construct validity of the scales of the LNNB—CR since tests supposedly assessing the same or similar skills tended to have higher coefficients (it should be noted that, in fact, this data could be used as construct validity evidence if the construct validity of the Halstead-Reitan subtests with this population has been well established). Berg et al. (1984) found a 91% agreement between the LNNB—CR and the Halstead-Reitan in terms of detection of cerebral dysfunction with a group of brain-damaged children.

Tramontana et al. (1983) examined the relationship between the LNNB—CR and the WISC—R. The sample consisted of 59 child and adolescent psychiatric patients, who were administered the LNNB—CR and the WISC—R. Correlations among the variables ranged from .01 to −.66. The correlations among the 11 LNNB—CR scales with the WISC—R Full Scale IQ were all statistically significant and ranged in value from .38 to −.63.

The LNNB—CR has also been correlated with the Peabody Picture Vocabulary Test—Revised (PPVT—R) with normal children

(Quattrocchi & Golden, 1983). A group of 86 children with no history of brain damage, emotional disturbance, birth trauma, or physical handicaps were used in this study. The results indicated significant correlations between the PPVT—R and the Visual, Receptive Speech, Arithmetic, Memory, and Intelligence scales of the LNNB—CR. While the magnitude of these correlations is not great, they still suggest that the abilities assessed on these LNNB—CR scales are similar to the receptive language abilities assessed by the PPVT—R. Hence this finding casts some doubt on how discrete the LNNB—CR scales may be in assessing uniquely different abilities.

The development of new scales with LNNB—CR was the focus of another study (Sawicki, Leark, Golden, & Karras, 1984). The goal of this study was to derive and validate Pathognomonic, Left Sensorimotor, and Right Sensorimotor scales with the LNNB—CR. Two samples were used—one to derive the scales and one for validation. The procedure involved comparisons on all 149 items between normals and brain-damaged children with the validational sample. The 40 items which had the highest statistical values were then used in a discriminant analysis. This analysis identified 18 variables which best discriminated between the groups. Further item analysis was completed and 13 items identified, which comprised the Pathognomonic scale. The items for the Left and Right Sensorimotor scales were selected from items that call for lateralized performance. The authors state that items which lowered the internal consistency and/or reliability of a scale were not included. The performance on these scales by normal and brain-damaged children was then compared with the validational sample. The results indicated statistically significant differences between the groups on all the scales. Discriminant analysis for both samples indicated that the Pathognomonic scale contributed the most variance (using all the scales of the LNNB—CR) to the analysis, and that both the Left and Right Sensorimotor scales were likewise significant.

FINDINGS WITH LEARNING-DISABLED CHILDREN

There has been considerable research examining the LNNB—CR with learning-disabled children. In general, the data suggest that the battery is effective at discriminating normals from LD children

(Geary & Gilger, 1984; Geary, Jennings, Schultz, & Alper, 1984; Nolan, Hammeke, & Barkley, 1983). Geary and Gilger (1984) compared LD with normal children who had been matched on Full Scale IQ. The groups differed significantly on the following four LNNB—CR scales: Rhythm, Expressive Speech, Writing, and Reading. Geary and colleagues (1984) examined the utility of the regression formula criteria for differentiating LD from normal children. These authors considered a normal profile as less than two T-scores above the regression value, a borderline profile as two T-scores above the regression value with one of those scales being either Writing or Arithmetic, and an abnormal profile as three or more scales above the regression value or two scales above the value excluding Writing and Arithmetic. They felt that borderline and abnormal profiles were indicative of a learning disability and a normal profile would not indicate LD. Using this criterion, all of the LD children were correctly identified and two false positives identified in the normal group.

Nolan et al. (1983) compared patterns on the LNNB—CR with groups of LD and normal children. The sample consisted of 36 children separated into one of three groups (normal control group, reading- and spelling-disabled group, and math-disabled group). The normal control group comprised children whose grade equivalent scores on the WRAT were at or above the 40th percentile. The reading- and spelling-disabled group consisted of children whose reading and spelling scores on the WRAT were at or below the 20th percentile but whose arithmetic scores were above the 40th percentile. The math-disabled group comprised children whose WRAT arithmetic scores were at or below the 20th percentile but whose reading and spelling scores were at or above the 40th percentile. The groups were compared on both the WISC—R and the LNNB—CR. These results indicated that the normal control group scored significantly higher on Verbal and Full Scale IQ than both the LD groups. There were no significant differences among the groups on Performance IQ or between the LD groups on Verbal and Full Scale IQ. Using Full Scale IQ and age as covariates, results for the LNNB—CR indicated that there was a significant difference among the groups on the Expressive Speech, Writing, and Reading scales. Follow-up pairwise comparisons showed the normal control group and the math-disabled group to be significantly better on the three scales than the reading- and spelling-disabled group. There were no significcant differences between the normal control and math-disabled children. Thus, it would appear that the LNNB—CR is particularly sensitive to semantic-linguistic deficits as might be evidenced by the reading- and spelling-disabled children, and less sensitive to the deficits (according to Rourke & Finlayson, 1978) that math-disabled children might evidence in visual-spatial processing. The assumption, of course, is that neurological deficits disrupt optimal functioning of the semantic-linguistic system in most learning-disabled children.

The LD-normal comparisons with the LNNB—CR provide some supportive data for the discriminative validity of this test, although less favorable results are reported with other LD studies (Snow & Hynd, 1985a, b; Snow, Hynd, & Hartlage, 1984; Snow, Hartlage, Hynd, & Grant, 1983). Snow and his colleagues (1983) correlated the LNNB—CR with the Minnesota Percepto-Diagnostic Test (MPD) with a group of LD children. The results indicated low to moderate correlations among the scales of the LNNB—CR but no significant correlation among any of the scales with the MPD. In this study, the important features seem to be the weaknesses of the LNNB—CR in assessing visual-motor abilities and the fact that the MPD was corrected for both age and IQ. The influence of IQ level with the LNNB—CR was demonstrated in another LD study (Snow, Hynd, & Hartlage, 1984), which examined differences in performance on the LNNB—CR between mildly and more severely LD children. Initial analysis indicated that the two groups differed significantly on 4 of the 11 scales (Receptive Speech, Writing, Reading, Arithmetic), with the severely LD group exhibiting a more impaired performance. However, there were no differences between the groups when WISC—R Full Scale IQ and WRAT achievement scores were used as covariates, suggesting a strong relationship between performance on the LNNB—CR and general ability.

The factor structure of the LNNB—CR as well as subgrouping analysis have also been examined with the battery (Snow & Hynd, 1985a, b). Snow and Hynd (1985a) conducted an across-scales factor analysis with the LNNB—CR. The results indicated a three-factor solution. The first factor had high to moderate loadings from six scales (Visual, Receptive Speech, Expressive Speech, Arithmetic, Memory, and Intellectual Processes) and was interpreted as representing a Language-General Intelligence Factor. The second factor had high loadings from the Writing and Reading Scales and was interpreted as representing a General Academic Achievement factor.

The third factor had moderate to high loadings from three scales (Motor, Rhythm, and Tactile) and was interpreted as representing a Sensory-Motor factor.

In a second study, Snow and Hynd (1985b) examined the effectiveness of the LNNB—CR in differentiating subgroups of LD children. The 11 scales of the LNNB—CR were utilized in a Q-technique factor analysis and three subgroups emerged. The subgroups had very similar patterns and did not differ on WISC—R and WRAT achievement scores (with the exception that there was a significant difference between two of the subgroups on WRAT spelling). In general, these results suggest that the scales of the LNNB—CR assess limited abilities (particularly visual-spatial) with LD children, and that the effect of general ability on performance on the LNNB—CR is very marked.

CONCLUSIONS

Data for the LNNB—CR point toward cautious use of this test. The battery does appear to be effective in discriminating brain-damaged from normals as well as LDs from normals (Carr, Sweet, Rossini, & Angara, 1983). However, there is little evidence as to the construct validity for the test, particularly with brain-damaged and normal children. Put simply, there are few data that correlate the performance of children with documented (e.g., CT scan) and localized damage (e.g., left temporal) on particular items or scales (e.g., receptive speech). Those few studies that have attempted to compare performance on the LNNB—CR and the Halstead-Reitan Batteries (e.g., Berg et al., 1984; Tramontana et al., 1983; Tramontana et al., 1984) have yielded promising results. However, similar and more sophisticated efforts are needed.

Data with LD children suggest that only a few scales are effective in differentiating them from normals or among LD subgroups. These scales appear to be the language and academic achievement subtests, abilities which are probably already adequately assessed by most standard evaluation procedures and instruments.

In general, it is felt that the primary concern with the LNNB—CR is the quantitative scales. The scales are heterogeneous in nature, and the clinician should use the scores for basic general decisions (e.g., brain-damaged profile or non-brain-damaged profile). Moving beyond this, the clinician should focus on item as well as qualitative error analysis as endorsed by Golden (1981). The LNNB—CR has a number of excellent items which can provide important and useful neuropsychological information.

Data in support of the conclusion that the 11 scales are heterogeneous in nature is derived from a recently conducted large-scale factor analytic study (Karras, Newlin, Franzen, Golden, Wilkening, Rothermel, & Tramontana, 1987). These investigators examined the factor structure of the LNNB—CR in a population of 719 children (240 normal, 253 brain-damaged, 32 suspected brain damage, 39 learning-disabled, 5 leukemic, and 150 psychiatric cases).

Factor analysis employing the 149 items from the protocols of these cases resulted in 11 internally consistent factors which, to some extent, were reflective of the organization of the battery. Of the 149 items on the LNNB—CR, 75 loaded independently on the 11 factors. The remaining items loaded on factors that were not retained in the analysis or loaded on several factors.

The 11 factors that emerged from this analysis suggest several conclusions. First, the 11 scales of the LNNB—CR are redundant and only about half (75 out of 149) of the items load significantly on factors reflecting more or less independent abilities. Second, since this battery generally requires from 1.5 to 2.5 hours to administer, might it not be wiser to only administer those items loading on the 11 factors? This would reduce administration time which would be advantageous for referred children who frequently have attentional problems and, perhaps, would provide more meaningful data from a neuropsychological perspective. And, third, the factor scores may provide better differentiation between normal-pathological samples.

Recognizing this potential use, Karras et al. (1987) derived T-scores for the 11 factors from the 240 normals and computed factor T-scores for the normals, psychiatric, and brain-damaged groups. Multiple ANOVAS revealed significant differences across these groups on 10 factors. The three groups failed to be distinguished from each other on a factor measuring drawing time.

This report is potentially important to those who choose to use the LNNB—CR in clinical practice. It may well be of potential benefit to compute factor scores which may have potentially greater utility in clinical diagnosis than the test's scales, since some research suggests that the scales are of little value in distinguishing children with different clinical disorders (Schaughency, Lahey, Hynd, Stone, &

TABLE 5.2

LNNB—CR Factors As Reported by Karras and Colleagues (1987)[a]

Factor	Descriptor	Item nos.
1.	Academic Skills	116, 115, 92, 118, 105, 117, 112, 119, 124, 121, 111, 110, 91, 120, 106, & 126
2.	Spatial Integration	11, 12, 149, 65, 79, & 127
3.	Spatially Based Movement	4, 14, 13, 5, 6, & 7
4.	Motor Speed	3, 1, 2, 17, 16, & 15
5.	Drawing Quality	29, 27, 23, 25, 31, & 21
6.	Drawing Time	24, 30, 26, 32, 28, & 22
7.	Rhythm Perception & Reproduction	42, 41, 40, & 39
8.	Somatosensory	51, 52, 44, 43, 47, 48, 45, & 46
9.	Receptive Language	67, 69, 68, 71, & 75
10.	Expressive Speech	84, 85, 86, 83, 87, 88, 94, & 89
11.	Abstract Verbal Reasoning	145, 144, 142, & 147

[a] Items per factor are listed in order of their loading on that particular factor.

Piacentini, 1988). Caution should be exercised in this regard, though, because the concerns Spiers (1982) and Stambrook (1983) have expressed may also be relevant to the study done by Karras and his colleagues (1987). Table 5.2 notes the LNNB—CR items that load significantly on these 11 factors.

The potential utility of the special scales (e.g., Pathognomonic, Left and Right Sensorimotor), critical level regression formula, and 11 factor scores need to be established in not only normal, brain-damaged and learning-disabled populations, but also with regard to other clinical groups, such as children with hyperactivity, various genetic disorders (e.g., Turner's Syndrome) and, generally, in conditions presumed to have a neurological etiology. At present, the data provided by the 11 scales are redundant to a significant degree when compared with that provided by traditional cognitive, academic, and perceptual motor assessment procedures which characterize much of clinical practice with children (Tuma & Pratt, 1982).

6

AN ECLECTIC APPROACH TO NEUROPSYCHOLOGICAL ASSESSMENT WITH CHILDREN

For a neuropsychological test battery to be maximally useful, it needs to be capable of diagnosing the location and approximate size of a lesion, the probable cause of the lesion, and the severity of impairment incurred. Such a battery should include tests that are sensitive to the general adequacy of brain functions as well as the integrity of specific parts of the brain.

—Selz, 1981

From the two preceding chapters on the Halstead-Reitan batteries and the Luria-Nebraska Neuropsychological Battery—Children's Revision, it should be clear that these lengthy batteries offer both comfort and concern for the clinician. Both of these approaches to assessment evaluate abilities that seem to provide adequate discrimination between children with brain damage and those without known pathology. Further, they provide what would appear to be adequate differentiation between normal children and those suffering learning disabilities.

While these batteries and the many studies summarized in Appendix A and B provide some assurance that the administration of one of these batteries will help in differential diagnosis, a critical use is nonetheless cautioned. Problems shared by these batteries include: (1) inadequate normative base, (2) very significant influence of general ability on the test results, (3) inadequate evidence of content validity, and (4) homogeneous scales and measures. Further, each of these batteries inadequately assesses some relevant domain of neuropsychological functioning. The Halstead-Reitan Batteries poorly assess verbal-linguistic abilities and the LNNB—CR is inadequate in its appraisal of perceptual-motor abilities. The LNNB—CR can also be criticized because even the motor or perceptual tasks may involve complex verbal directions—potentially a very significant problem for a child with a serious language disorder.

Finally, there exists no convincing evidence that these batteries offer any more discrete measures of neuropsychological functioning than traditional clinical or psychoeducational evaluations. Consider, for example, the factoral study conducted by Crockett et al. (1969) on the Reitan-Indiana Battery. Those factors accounting for the most variance were: (1) a perceptual-analytic factor, (2) a motor-speed factor, and (3) a verbal-concept formation factor.

A recent factor analytic study of psychoeducational evaluations by Sutter, Bishop and Battin (1986) revealed a similar factor structure. In this study five factors were found including: (1) language factor, (2) academic achievement factor, (3) visual-spatial factor, (4) attention and memory factor, and (5) motor-speed factor.

An alternative to employing a standardized neuropsychological battery is to develop an eclectic approach to clinical child neuropsychological assessment. Such an approach allows several advantages. For example, rather than giving the same lengthy battery to each child regardless of the referral questions, a uniquely suited battery of measures can be selected and given to each child which, presumably, will assess the specific deficit suspected and answer the referral question very directly. Also, highly redundant measures can be eliminated, thereby shortening the evaluation session. For brain-damaged children, who frequently have a low frustration tolerance and may be distractible and hyperactive, such a goal has obvious advantages. Also, with a shorter, more referral-oriented battery selected by the examiner, time may permit more behavioral measures of adaptive behavior, emotional adjustment, and peer-social status. Because none of the batteries reviewed in the foregoing chapters incorporate measures of emotional adjustment, the latter must be administered after the standardized battery is completed. Finally, by employing an eclectic approach to neuropsychological assessment, one can select more psychometrically sound measures than may be included in the standardized battery. For example, the Wide Range Achievement Test—Revised is administered as part of the Halstead-

Reitan batteries. While this measure may be a good screening measure of academic proficiency, it has yet to receive a favorable review and reviewers consistently caution against its use as a measure of academic achievement (Matuszek, 1985; Saigh, 1985).

There is no correct approach to neuropsychological assessment with adults or children. Each approach has its advantages or disadvantages. Luria's qualitative, non-normed, and dynamic assessment approach, for example, may be an excellent approach with adults where age norms are not so essential. It would be completely inappropriate with children since, without age norms or a standardized format, one cannot know whether poor performance is due to developmental delay, brain damage, or variation in administration procedures.

The following eclectic model and approach employs, or recommends, a wide range of possible clinical and psychometric instruments. It would be up to the knowledgeable clinician to design an assessment approach from such a model which would be appropriate for the child, aimed at answering the referral question, and economical in its time requirements. At a minimum, probably two measures per domain (except perhaps in the cognitive domain) should be selected.

AN ECLECTIC MODEL

Obrzut (1981) has provided a potentially valuable framework for conceptualizing neuropsychological assessment with a child who has been referred for an evaluation. He proposes that learning and behavior may be viewed as a hierarchy of information processing. As outlined by Johnson and Myklebust (1967) this hierarchy involves sensation, perception, memory, symbolization, and conceptualization. To this framework one might add motor functioning to perception since, for example, motoric ability provides kinesthetic feedback and serves as a basis for perceptual learning. Within this context it is important to realize that being hierarchic in nature, any deficit or disability acquired at one level will affect development of abilities at other, higher levels of cognitive functioning. Deficient performance on perceptual tasks will thus likely affect memory, symbolization, and conceptualization.

It is within this framework that neuropsychological assessment with children might best be conceptualized. Recognized and validated clinical assessment procedures pertinent to abilities and skills within each of these hierarchic levels of information processing can be incorporated within the clinical assessment. In this manner the clinician is not tied to a set neuropsychological battery that may be inappropriate for a particular child; instead, the clinician may utilize assessment instruments both pertinent to a particular child and to a child's other needs, and use tests that he has found especially useful. The complete neuropsychological evaluation will still take between four to eight hours, usually covering an entire day. Needless to say, the amount of time any particular evaluation takes will depend greatly on the extent of the evaluation, the expertise of the examiner, the cooperation of the child and, of course, the time available to work with the child.

So that the possible context for the neuropsychological evaluation of the child can be determined, the following discussion will focus on the hierarchy of information processing noted earlier, together with possible tests appropriate to tap abilities at each level. The various tasks or tests suggested are only recommended. At least two points should be kept in mind. First, abilities at each level should be adequately assessed using at least two, if not more, correlated measures. In this fashion the probability of making errors in clinical judgment (i.e., diagnosing neuropsychological deficits when none exists) will be greatly reduced. If deficit performance on one task cannot be supported by equally deficient performance on some related (correlated) task, then a judgment regarding neuropsychological deficit should probably not be made. Considerable clinical expertise in neuropsychological assessment and diagnosis is, therefore, required to adequately conceptualize and describe the unique pattern of deficits found in each child evaluated. With these points in mind, it is now appropriate to discuss the framework for the neuropsychological battery.

Sensation and Sensory Recognition

Sensation refers to the lowest possible aspect of behavior in that sensory mechanisms appear to activate appropriately to stimulation. In many respects, it is difficult to differentiate sensation from perception since the two mechanisms are so closely tied. For our purpose we will consider lower levels of perception tied to sensory abilities.

In this framework it is imperative to attend to two basic processes associated with sensory abilities: acuity and recognition of sensation. The complete developmental and health history of the dyslexic child

TABLE 6.1
Conceptual Hierarchy of Neuropsychological Organization and
Measures of Value in Clinical Child Assessment*

Sensation and Sensory recognition

Acuity

  Visual Acuity
  Auditory Acuity
  Developmental and Health History

Recognition

  Finger Agnosia (Finger Localization)
  Finger-Tip Number Writing
  Single and Double Simultaneous (Face-Hand) Stimulation Test
  Tactile Form Recognition Test

Perception

Auditory

  Benton Phoneme Discrimination
  Speech Sounds Perception Test
  Seashore Rhythm Test
  Wepman Auditory Discrimination Test

Visual

  Bender Gestalt Test
  Berry Visual Motor Integration Test (VMI)
  Benton Visual Retention Test
  Benton Facial Recognition Test
  Benton Judgment of Line Orientation Test
  Benton Visual Form Discrimination

Tactile-Kinesthetic

  Tactual Performance Test (TPT)
  Tactile Form Recognition

Motor

Cerebellar Screening

  Tandem Walking (heel-to-toe)

TABLE 6.1 Continued

Finger to Nose to Examiner's Finger
Tests for Dysarthria
Tests for Nystagmus
Evaluation for Hypotonia

Lateral Dominance—Motor Only

Grip Strength
Edinburgh Inventory
Halstead-Reitan Lateral Dominance Examination
Finger Oscillation (Finger-Tapping) Test

Psycholinguistic

Screening Measures

Aphasia Screening Test
Boston Naming Test
Color Naming (Denckla)
Rapid Alternating Stimulus Naming
Fluency Test
Peabody Picture Vocabulary Test—Revised (PPVT—R)

Formal Batteries

Boston Diagnostic Aphasia Examination
Orzeck Aphasia Evaluation
Illinois Test of Psycholinguistic Ability (ITPA)
Northwestern Syntax Test

Language Asymmetries

Dichotic Listening Task
Visual Half-Field Technique
Time-Sharing Tasks

Academic (Reading)

Informal Batteries

Clinical Interview

Attitudes
Interests
Socialization
Self Concept

Test for Phonetic Sounds (nonsense words)
Test for Vowel Principles (nonsense words)

(Continued)

TABLE 6.1 Continued

Syllabication (nonsense words)
Informal Reading Inventory
Writing Sample
Spelling Test
Try-outs—Diagnostic Teaching

Formal Batteries

Learning Modalities

Mills Learning Methods Test
Detroit Tests of Learning Aptitude (Revised)
Illinois Test of Psycholinguistic Ability (ITPA)

Durrell Analysis of Reading Difficulties
Gates-McKillop Reading Diagnostic Test
Woodcock Reading Mastery Tests—Revised
Wide Range Achievement Test—Revised
Boder Diagnostic Reading-Spelling Test

Cognitive—Intellectual

Category Test
Raven's Colored Progressive Matrices Test
Kaufman Assessment Battery for Children (K-ABC)
McCarthy Scales of Children's Abilities (MSCA)
Wechsler Intelligence Scale of Intelligence—Revised (WISC—R)
Wechsler Preschool and Primary Scales of Intelligence

Behavioral/Affective

Achenbach Child Behavior Checklist
Children's Depression Inventory
Hopelessness Scale
Personality Inventory for Children
Revised Children's Manifest Anxiety Scale
Sociometric Class Exercise
Structured Child Psychiatric Interview
   (Multiple Informants)

* It should be emphasized that this conceptual hierarchy and the suggested assessment procedures are not meant to be all inclusive. The knowledgeable clinician should use his professional expertise in designing a comprehensive and individually appropriate neuropsychological battery in keeping with each child's unique needs. Modified from Hynd and Cohen, 1983, with permission.

is obviously important in that early deficits in the acuity of sensation may be reported. A child who seems unresponsive to loud noise as an infant and who has a history of early otitis media may evidence auditory sensory deficits. These behaviors are often associated with impaired speech and language (Katz, 1978; Needleman, 1977), behavioral problems (Hersher, 1978), and various learning disorders (Downs, 1977; Howie, 1977; Zinkus, Gottlieb, & Shapiro, 1978). Visual difficulties may similarly be manifested at an early age, thus making the careful taking of a developmental and health history even more important. It should also not be assumed that the child has adequate visual or auditory acuity simply because there is no history of problems suggestive of these difficulties. Unless there is evidence that hearing and vision have been checked, each child should receive a vision and hearing evaluation prior to the more formalized neuropsychological assessment.

Sensory recognition is a somewhat higher level of functioning, which admittedly involves basic perceptual processes. These basic perceptual processes are at such a low level that their inclusion is appropriate. It is here that basic recognition and awareness of sensory stimulation become apparent. As can be seen in Table 6.1, such tasks as Finger-Tip Number Writing, the Single and Double Simultaneous (Face-Hand) Stimulation Test (Centofanti & Smith, 1978), and the Tactile Form Recognition Test would be appropriate measures of sensory recognition. The Finger Agnosia Test (Gerstmann, 1924, 1930) has been controversial (Benton, 1955) but in many reports also seems to be sensitive to sensory dysfunction (K. Hermann, 1964; Kinsbourne & Warrington, 1963; Lindgren, 1978; Satz & Friel, 1973). In fact, in the study reported by Lindgren (1978) in which 100 kindergarten children were administered a test battery at the beginning of kindergarten and again at the end of first grade, assessed as to reading ability, it was concluded that in classifying the "sample of children as poor readers or as adequate readers [at the end of first grade] on the basis of FL [finger localization] performance alone results in correct classification for three out of four children" (p. 97). The complex nature of the finger agnosia task in terms of the functional system involved in sensory recognition makes it a potentially sensitive measure in reflecting significant neuropsychological deficits.

There are at least two considerations that should be pointed out. First, performance on the ability to localize which finger was touched by the examiner, as on the Finger Agnosia Test, should be considered in the light of right-sided/left-sided differences. Consistently poor right-sided performance on Finger Agnosia, on Tactile Form Recognition, or on the Single and Double Simultaneous (Face-Hand) Stimulation Test may indicate dysfunction on the contralateral side. A child with consistently poor right-sided sensory performance may well have neuropsychological deficits associated with higher cognitive processes important in language and reading acquisition, which we know in most individuals are also lateralized to the left cerebral cortex (Hynd & Hynd, 1984).

The second consideration concerns the modality in which the associated deficit manifests itself. Are only tactile-kinesthetic abilities affected or are basic auditory deficits also present? If the deficits appear only in the tactile-kinesthetic domain, one might suspect more parietal lobe dysfunction and, thus, look for other correlates of parietal lobe dysfunction that may be associated findings (e.g., inability to copy or to recognize geometric shapes). The fact that isolated deficits may appear is again relatively meaningless unless the deficits can be correlated in a meaningful fashion with other test data. It is for this reason that an in-depth understanding of the material presented in Chapters Two and Three is so critical. It is also for this reason that so many measures are typically administered in a comprehensive neuropsychological examination.

Perceptual Processes

Basic brain-behavior relations begin with perception, which involves the organization and integration of basic sensory stimulation (Obrzut, 1981). As with basic sensation, visual, auditory, and tactile-kinesthetic modalities are involved in the perceptual processes. Auditory, visual, and tactile-kinesthetic memory may also be involved in perceptual performance.

In the auditory domain, the Seashore Rhythm Test (Knights & Norwood, 1979) is a popular measure of the ability to differentiate like from dissimilar pairs of sounds. The test requires the ability to sustain attention, remain alert to incoming auditory stimuli, and make comparative judgments regarding competing rhythmic sequences.

Visual perception has typically received more attention in the neuropsychological examination than has assessment of auditory perception. This is probably due to the emphasis placed on higher levels of language processes in the information processing hierarchy.

In large part, the relative neglect of the assessment of formal auditory-perceptual processes at the lower levels is due to the fact that basic processes affected by auditory-perceptual processes will later be associated with performance at higher levels of information processing.

The Bender Gestalt Test is one of the tests most frequently administered by neuropsychologists (Craig, 1979) as well as by psychologists who work within the school system (Goh, Teslow, & Fuller, 1980). The ability to correctly copy the designs presented on stimuli cards seems to assess the integrity of the visual-spatial perceptual system in integrating and organizing stimuli. Poor performance on the Bender Gestalt may relate to developmental immaturity or may indicate subjects with parietal lobe dysfunction (Garron & Cheifetz, 1965), possibly right parietal lobe damage (Diller, Ben-Yishay, Gerstmann, Goodkin, Gordon, & Weinberg, 1974; Hirschenfang, 1960). Poor performance on the Bender can either be indicative of developmental delay or be due to cerebral dysfunction. It is for this reason that one must be familiar with appropriate norms (Koppitz, 1963) and the performance pattern indicative of cortical pathology. Usually, the older the child, the fewer errors that could occur. For a 12-year-old boy referred for evaluation of severe learning difficulties, 10 errors would thus be truly significant. Qualitative analysis of performance is also necessary in clinical diagnosis, since some copying errors are more indicative of cerebral dysfunction than are others.

Another popular test frequently used with children is the Developmental Test of Visual Motor Integration (VMI; Beery, 1974). Designed for preschool and elementary school children, the Berry VMI has been found to discriminate reasonably well between children who become fluent readers from those who later evidence reading problems (Lindgren, 1978). This test simply requires a child to copy a series of progressively more difficult geometric designs. Developmental aspects affecting performance again need to be considered along with possible indices of cortical dysfunction.

Within the tactile-kinesthetic realm, two measures seem particularly useful for assessment of the child. The Tactual Performance Test (TPT) is a modification of the Seguin-Goddard Formboard. Six forms are to be placed on a board by the child. The child is blindfolded prior to administration of the test, his hands run over the form outlines on the board, and the child is told to fit the forms in the proper spaces using only his preferred hand. The child then performs this task a second time using his non-preferred hand and, finally, a third time using both hands. The time required to complete the task with each hand may provide a good indicator of right-sided/left-sided performance. After the TPT board has been removed from sight, the child is asked to draw a diagram of the board, noting the proper location of each form. Three scores are considered in evaluating the TPT results: Time, Memory, and Localization. In addition to providing some data on right-left differences, the TPT assesses tactile-kinesthetic form discrimination, incidental spatial memory, spatial visualization, and tactile memory (Selz, 1981).

The Tactile Form Recognition Test is another relatively simple task to administer to a child. Four plastic forms (circle, square, triangle, and cross) are placed in the child's hand and must be matched against forms visually presented. Both errors and response time are recorded. This test can provide a good measure of parietal lobe functioning as well as data pertinent to right-sided/left-sided comparisons.

Benton, Hamsher, Varney, and Spreen (1983) have provided a particularly useful and well-validated set of visual-perceptual measures that have age norms for children (usually ages six to fourteen). The measures that may be of most clinical relevance here include the Facial Recognition Test and the Judgment of Line Orientation Test.

Motoric Evaluation

Conceptualization of the evaluation of the motor system should entail screening of cerebellar and motoric functioning and an evaluation of lateral motor dominance. The first component of the evaluation should be a screening for neurological integrity. If significant deficits are suspected, it may then be appropriate to refer to a neurologist. This also applies should a suspicion exist that deterioration or cerebellar disease may be present. The second aspect of the motoric evaluation is to determine both the preferences and the levels of lateralized motor performance. Such an evaluation can indicate contralateral cortical dysfunction or weak preference patterns which may be identified in the dyslexic child.

Cerebellar Functioning

DeMyer (1974) has noted that there are many misunderstandings regarding what the cerebellum actually does. He quotes Laurence Sterne (1713–1768), who satirized the "speculative neurophysiology" that was popular in the eighteenth century.

> But how great was his apprehension, when he farther understood, that [the force of Paturition] acting upon the very vertex of the head, not only injured the brain itself, or cerebrum,—but that it necessarily squeezed and propelled the cerebrum towards the cerebellum, which was the immediate seat of the understanding!—Angeles and ministers of grace defend us! cried my father,—can any soul withstand this shock?—No wonder the intellectual web is so rent and tattered as we see it; and that so many of our best heads are no better than a puzzled skein of silk,—all perplexity,—all confusion within—side. (From *The Life and Opinions of Tristain Shandy Gentleman* as quoted by DeMyer, 1974, p. 237)

The cerebellum working in concert with the pons coordinates posture, muscle movement sense, and controls and refines motor movements. Unfortunately, it is not the "seat of understanding!" Dysarthria, nystagmus, and hypotonia are considered to be clinical signs of cerebellar dysfunction. Children or adults who manifest clinical signs of dystaxia resemble a person who is intoxicated. They typically have difficulty standing on one foot and sway and stagger when walking. Tandem walking (or walking heel-to-toe) often elicits dystaxic behavior. Dystaxia-dysmetria of the arm can also be elicited by asking the child to touch his nose and then touch the examiner's finger, which is moving in an arc approximately one foot from the face of the child. A child who evidences dysmetria often undershoots or overshoots the target because he poorly esti-mates the distance and arc between his nose and the examiner's finger. This performance results from dysequilibrium of contractions of the muscles or, as DeMyer (1974) states, "the agonist-antagonist contractions which arrest movement" (p. 244).

Dysarthria can be elicited or noted on tests of higher cognitive functions and should be apparent on the Aphasia Screening Test, or more comprehensive aphasia diagnostic exams (e.g., Boston Diag-nostic Aphasia Examination, Orzeck Aphasia Evaluation), or on oral reading tests in which slurred speech may be evident. Nystagmus, or jerky eye movements, may be associated with cerebellar dys-function or may be due to the close relationship the pathways have to other brain stem structures. Nystagmus may result from lesions of the eye, the vestibular system, or other brain-stem lesions. It can be elicited by asking the child to slowly follow the examiner's finger with his eyes. The child's head should remain stationary while this task is executed. If nystagmus is found in screening, there is no reason to refer the child to a neurologist unless the symptoms have an acute onset, are associated with nausea (with or without vomiting), vertigo is experienced, and/or oscillopsia (oscillating vision) is present. The congenital nystagmus often found in dyslexic children (or children with other learning disabilities) is usually asymptomatic (DeMyer, 1974).

The child evidencing hypotonia gives the impression of a rag doll. The arms and feet seem floppy and he may look somewhat out of control when he walks. Passive movement of the arms or legs will reveal poor muscle tone for the child's age.

Lateral Dominance

In this component of the neuropsychological examination, it is important to evaluate performance in at least two dimensions. First, the level of performance itself is important since the implications on some tests of depressed bilateral performance are different from that of unilaterally depressed performance. In concert with this notion is the idea of comparing right-sided versus left-sided performance.

The Grip Strength Test simply assesses the child's grip strength as evidenced on a dynamometer. Using the Smedley Hand Dynamometer, a child is allowed two trials for each hand. Grip strength is measured in kilograms and the score is the average of the two trials per hand. As with Finger Oscillation (Finger-Tapping), Finger Localization, and Finger-Tip Number Writing, normative data are provided for males and females, aged six through fourteen. The vast majority of children should show a strong right-sided preference. Unilaterally, poor performance may be associated with cortical dysfunction in the contralateral cerebral hemisphere.

The Finger Oscillation Test assesses motor speed on a manual finger tapper. The child rests his or her hand on a board and taps the tapper key as fast as possible for 10 seconds. Five 10-second trials are given for each hand, using the index finger to depress the key. The score reported is the average number of taps for each hand over the 10-second trials. Similar to the Grip Strength Test, finger oscillation provides a good indication of the contralateral motor cortex for the child.

The Edinburgh Inventory (Oldfield, 1971) and the Halstead-Reitan Lateral Dominance Examination provide a good indication of a child's preferences on lateral motor tasks. Simply stated, mixed or weak preferences on lateralized tasks are often found in children who have behavioral or learning problems but they are not correlated directly with academic or intellectual abilities (Hynd, Obrzut, & Obrzut, 1981). It is important, therefore, to assess lateral dominance but, since it represents an ability that may or may not be involved in the neuropsychological profile of a specific child, one should be cautious about drawing conclusions regarding cognitive functioning.

Up to this point we have discussed in rather specific terms the various tests or tasks associated with the assessment of basic sensory, perceptual, and motor abilities which serve as a foundation for the development of higher cognitive functioning. It has been proposed that there is a great likelihood that deficits or dysfunctional abilities at these lower levels may adversely affect learning and performance. This proposal is not absolute since there are children with mild cerebral palsy who suffer only motor dysfunction and who seem to have more than adequate cognitive abilities. The probability that deficits associated with audition and vision will affect language learning, however, is greater than with deficits in the motor systems since these two basic sensory/perceptual processes are directly involved in most higher cognitive functions. It is once again stressed that differential diagnosis must involve the articulation of indices of cortical dysfunction with the pattern of deficits on cognitive tasks as they relate to our understanding of the functional system of behavior.

Since the last three aspects of our information processing hierarchy—memory, symbolization, and conceptualization—are so closely intertwined, they will be considered within the context of recognized components of assessment of higher cortical function as pertinent to the evaluation of the child. The following discussion will be organized into three broad categories: evaluation of psycholinguistic functioning, assessment of academic abilities (primarily reading), and evaluation of cognitive intellectual processing abilities.

Psycholinguistic Functioning

As used in the context of this chapter, an assessment of psycholinguistic functioning entails more than simply the ability to use speech and language. It encompasses the ability to use speech and language in a meaningful and socially acceptable fashion; it relates speech and language to the psychological processes that are inherent in articulating meaningful concepts. Psycholinguistic evaluation should thus examine not only the very basic abilities associated with language, but should also qualitatively relate speech and language capabilities to age-appropriate behavior.

The Aphasia Screening Test and the Fluency Test provide good screening measures that may indicate whether more thorough in-depth evaluations are in order. More often than not, a formalized assessment of psycholinguistic abilities should be carried out with a subject, unless it is believed that other measures associated with academic and cognitive assessment will reveal similar information. The Aphasia Screening Test resulted from Reitan's revision of the Halstead-Wepman Aphasia Screening Test (Halstead & Wepman, 1949). Its primary purpose is to identify language-based disorders that may be manifested on spelling, reading, arithmetic, articulation, and orientation tasks (Selz, 1981). A number of studies (e.g., Teeter, 1983) have suggested that the Aphasia Screening Test is an excellent screening measure in identifying children who have neuropsycho-logically based disorders.

The Fluency Test simply requires the child to name as many words as possible in 60 seconds. For more fluent individuals (such as older adolescents or adults) the task can be made more difficult by asking them to name as many words as they can that begin with a specific letter, such as "e," in 60 seconds. The Peabody Picture Vocabulary Test—Revised (PPVT—R) has been shown to be especially useful with children suspected of having receptive language difficulties (Zaidel, 1976).

The various aphasia test batteries, such as the Boston Diagnostic Aphasia Examination or the Orzeck Aphasia Evaluation (Orzeck, 1966), are more appropriate for older adolescents who suffer signi-ficant speech and language difficulties. These batteries typically assess for fluency, naming, repetition, paraphasias, and other char-acteristics often associated with aphasia. An important factor to consider is that since these batteries are so complete the results can be useful in conceptualizing cognitive deficits in the functional system that are believed to be associated with reading. Many of the tasks included on these batteries have been shown to correlate well with deficient left temporal and parietal lobe functioning (Frisch & Handler, 1974; McFie, 1960; Swiercinsky, 1979). Figure 2.3 shows the related neurolinguistic system.

At this point in the evaluation it might be meaningful to look at the relationship psycholinguistic functioning has to measures of language asymmetry. The dichotic listening and visual half-field paradigms may reveal important data about asymmetries in language processing (i.e., Does a strong right-ear effect exist? Do normal visual half-field asymmetries exist?) as well as revealing how efficient the language processor is in relation to indices of psycholinguistic abilities. For a child who has evidenced expressive and receptive speech deficits including poor oral fluency, anomia, and deficient phonetic analysis of unknown words, for example, it would not be unusual to find overall depressed dichotic listening performance in both ears or, more typically, poor recognition of dichotically presented stimuli to the right ear. A right-ear effect on a dichotic task is often thought to reflect left-cerebral hemispheric dominance for language. Since the dichotic listening task and visual half-field paradigms involve rather complex theoretical as well as practical issues, the reader may wish to refer to Kinsbourne and Hiscock (1981) for a detailed discussion.

In concluding this brief section on psycholinguistic assessment as part of a comprehensive neuropsychological evaluation of children, a few points need to be made. First, the relatively subtle deficits that children may show on these possible evaluation instruments argue strongly that one should not attempt to localize a lesion site. This makes not only good clinical sense but is also dictated by a knowledge of the aphasia literature. It has been realized over time that many subtypes of aphasia exist which are difficult to diagnose. It is known, furthermore, that the localization of expressive and receptive language deficits may occasionally involve the "minor" hemisphere in some cases and various subcortical structures in still others (April & Han, 1980; Kirshner & Kistler, 1982; Naeser, Alexander, Helm-Estabrooks, Levine, Laughlin, & Geschwind, 1982; Silverberg & Gordon, 1979).

Finally, it would appear that it is important, especially with children suspected of having neuropsychologically based learning problems, that one of the best discriminators of children with verbal deficits is performance on rapid alternating stimulus naming tasks (Wolf, 1986). Presumably, deficits in rapidly naming alternating stimuli (e.g., colors, numbers, letters) reflects an underlying deficit in automaticity which may characterize children with developmental learning, usually reading, problems (Wolf, Bally, & Morris, 1986).

Academic Achievement

Many of the readers of this volume will be most familiar with the realm of the assessment of academic and cognitive intellectual functioning. Studies have consistently shown that these domains are more frequently evaluated by specialists working with children. For this reason, not every possible assessment technique or evaluation method noted in Table 6.1 will be discussed in detail. Instead the focus is on those techniques which are often overlooked or are less frequently used as part of the clinical assessment.

Informal Evaluation

The clinical interview can be one of the most productive encounters between the examiner and child. During the interview the examiner can follow up tentative hypotheses formulated from reading the referral, from reading the developmental/health history, or from discussing the child with the parent. It is often productive to first interview the parent(s) and the child together so that the child is able to know with certainty some of the perceptions of the parent(s) prior to being interviewed separately. When the child is interviewed alone, it is critical to gain some understanding as to how he perceives himself and his problem, to determine his attitudes and interests, to assess his feelings toward peers, and to gain an overall picture of his self-concept.

An understanding of the child's interests and attitudes is obviously important. First, it is vital to determine if a more formalized evaluation of emotionality and behavior needs to be conducted. If emotional problems are even suspected, a thorough evaluation must be conducted.

The purpose of informal assessment is to determine how the child actually reads by observing the child reading. The Slosson Oral Reading Test or Dolch Word List may be used, for example, in determining an appropriate entry level for the administration of an Informal Reading Inventory, which may be used to measure oral reading competency and silent and oral comprehension. Observation of the error patterns on tests for phonetic sounds and vowel principles using nonsense words (to avoid the confounding effect of previous learning) as well as a qualitative evaluation of errors on a free-writing sample or on a spelling test can reveal a great deal regarding the nature and patterns of reading errors. Unfortunately, psychologists typically have little training in this area. It is for this reason that a comprehensive neuropsychological evaluation that encompasses a detailed academic assessment might best be conducted by a multidisciplinary team. In this fashion, neuropsychological knowledge might be more closely matched with principles and practices of education diagnosis and intervention. Needless to say, such an approach would only be relevant if academic concerns initiated the referral.

Formal Batteries

Formal assessment tests or batteries offer potentially less specific clinical information on how a child actually reads, but they do have the advantage of examining recognized components of the reading process. Items such as word and letter recognition, sight vocabulary, word-attack skills, reading comprehension, and use of contextual cues can be assessed in a quantitative manner, thereby allowing a child's performance to be compared with either local norms or the performance of some other, more general reference group. The standard scores, percentiles, grade equivalent scores, and derived stanine scores can all be useful in charting a profile of a child's reading abilities. The Durrell Analysis of Reading Difficulties, Gates-McKillop Reading Diagnostic Test, and Woodcock Reading Mastery Tests—Revised are especially valuable in pinpointing specific areas of strength or weaknesses in reading.

An evaluation of preferred learning modalities is considered critical if one is to adequately match aptitudes and treatments (Reynolds, 1981). The Mills Learning Methods Test, the Detroit Tests of Learning Aptitude, and even the ITPA can be very useful in this regard. Strengths in visual or auditory channels or even the tactile channel as measured by the Mills Learning Methods Test can be useful in helping to maximize potential achievement. This seems particularly important in assisting the severely handicapped child (Wilson, 1981). Since the process of reading and, especially, the learning-to-read aspect may involve the differential use of preferred modalities (Bakker, 1981), clinicians need to be cautious in their conclusions and, due to the developmental nature of variations in preferred learning modalities, a constant monitoring should take place to ensure accurate conclusions regarding preferred learning modalities.

Cognitive-Intellectual Processes

The evaluation of higher cognitive processes from a neuropsychological point of view represents one of the greatest challenges and potential pitfalls if one is attempting to relate recognized cognitive processes to functional neuroanatomy. It will be recalled that Gall believed intelligence was localized in the frontal lobes, based primarily on his observations of his students (Pirozzolo, 1979). Since we know that basic life-sustaining functions, basic perceptual processes, and even expressive speech are relatively localized within the functional geography of the brain, it is tempting to relate and project our perceptions in this regard on higher mental processes. The localization of intellectual processes is unfortunately not a reality that can be said to exist. Luria's concept of a functional system is most relevant to our discussion here (Luria, 1980, pp. 32–33).

> If the higher mental functions are complex, organized functional systems that are social in origin, any attempt to localize them in special circumscribed areas ["centers"] of the cerebral cortex is even less justifiable than the attempt to seek narrow circumscribed "centers" for biological functional systems. The modern view regarding the possible localization of the higher mental functions is that they have a wide, dynamic representation throughout the cerebral cortex based on constellations of territorially scattered groups of "synchronously working ganglion cells, mutually exciting one another." (Ukhtomskii, 1945)

If higher mental functions (i.e., IQ) have a dynamic representation throughout the cortex, then it makes conceptual sense that while IQ might be affected by brain damage, in no way can it be concluded that IQ measures can be used to differentiate "right- versus left-brained thinkers" or, for example, that performance on one subtest on the WISC—R can definitively reveal deficits in right parietal lobe function. It is argued that correlations or relationships may exist between performance on various subtests of IQ tests and cortical deficits, but that due to psychometric issues (Kaufman, 1979), conceptual problems, and a basic understanding of Luria's theory, it is best to use IQ tests and other tests of higher cortical functioning as overall measures of the intactness of higher mental processes. Coupled with information gleaned from other sources and from assessing different aspects of lower level functioning, it may be appropriate to hypothesize about the site of cortical lesions in adults or in cases of children known to suffer brain damage. With school-age children referred for an in-depth neuropsychological evaluation of learning problems, however, it is argued that it is inappropriate to attempt a diagnosis of the site of cortical dysfunction.

The Category Test (from the Halstead Battery) consists of 168 consecutively presented slides. The slides are projected on an opaque screen and four numbered levers appear below the screen.

The child looks at the stimulus projected onto the screen and depresses one of the four numbered levers. Immediate feedback is provided to the child. A bell indicates the selection of a correct choice, while a buzzer indicates an incorrect choice. The next slide automatically appears on the screen after the feedback. Six groups of slides exist, each group having an underlying principle governing the correct response. It is the child's task to learn the principles based on their experience. The Category Test is believed to assess the ability to reason abstractly and form concepts. It also measures the child's ability to learn from experience and shift conceptual sets. It is considered, by and large, to be a good measure of intellectual and cognitive ability.

The Raven's Coloured Progressive Matrices Test, originally conceived and developed in England, is a multiple-choice paper-and-pencil test for children five to eleven years of age. Similar to the Category Test, it is thought to be culturally more fair than many traditional intelligence tests (e.g., Stanford-Binet, WISC—R). It takes about 45 minutes and simply requires the child to match a nonrepresentational colored pattern with a correct choice. While the Raven's Coloured Progressive Matrices Test seems to be a relatively good measure of overall ability, it nevertheless correlates with educational level and has nonstratified norms. While this test may be a good general measure of simple and complex reasoning skills, it should probably be used only as an adjunct measure of ability.

The test of intellectual ability that has received the greatest attention by far is the WISC—R. Divided into two subscales, the subtests of the WISC—R provide Verbal, Performance, and Full Scale IQ scores. While a great amount of research appears to have been done relating performance on the Wechsler Intelligence Scale for Adults (WAIS) to localized brain dysfunction, little has been done along this line with the WISC—R. As discussed earlier in this volume, evidence does exist that the left hemisphere is responsible for analytic, sequential, and language processing. The right cerebral hemisphere seems more responsible for gestalt propositional processing (Bogen, 1969, 1975; Gazzaniga, 1975). It, therefore, seems a reasonable assumption that the Verbal Scale IQ score should reflect left hemisphere functioning while the Performance Scale IQ should reflect the integrity of the right cerebral hemisphere. While there is certainly some correlative evidence that suggests this may be the case (Fedio & Mirsky, 1969; Rourke, Young, & Flewelling, 1971), the fact is that the difficulty in finding children with circumscribed lateralized lesions has precluded any definitive statements in this regard (Reed, 1976). Once again it seems prudent, therefore, to consider the preferred mode of processing information as being diagnostically more meaningful. Bannatyne (1971, 1974) originally proposed a recategorization of the WISC—R subtests into a more meaningful framework. Using his categorization scheme, children with severe reading failure did best on subtests assessing spatial ability and poorest on subtests assessing sequencing skills (Arithmetic, Digit Span, and Coding; Rugel, 1974). Successive processing is exactly what it implies. Information is processed temporally and may be affected by damage to the frontal and temporal lobes. Simultaneous processing, on the other hand, involves gestalt-like processing in which information is processed as a whole. Occipitoparietal dysfunction may disrupt simultaneous processing. As Obrzut (1981) notes, the nature of the stimuli may be unrelated to the processing whereas, "verbal processing [is] . . . not necessarily associated with successive processing, and visual-spatial stimuli do not automatically demand simultaneous processing" (p. 261). Related to the WISC—R, simultaneous processing would be assessed by performance on the Picture Completion, Block Design, and Object Assembly subtests. Successive processing, on the other hand, could be inferred through a subject's performance on Picture Arrangement, Coding, and Mazes subtests. No matter what perspective is used in attempting to analyze WISC—R performance, the reader should focus on processing strategies that seem to relate to other neuropsychological test data and avoid the temptation to localize dysfunction based on WISC—R performance.

Other potentially useful measures of cognitive-intellectual functioning include the McCarthy Scales of Children's Abilities and the Kaufman Assessment Battery for Children (K-ABC). Research conducted by Kaufman, Kaufman, Kamphaus, and Naglieri (1982) and by Kamphaus, Kaufman, and Kaufman (1982) seem to support two robust factors, simultaneous and successive from age 2.5 years through 12.5 years. This test could be very useful in clinical child neuropsychology if future research with normal and brain-damaged children provides further evidence as to the K-ABC's construct validity and reliability. In one study (Hooper & Hynd, 1985) the K-ABC Scales provided excellent discrimination between normal and dyslexic children, but the discriminant ability of the test was poor in differentiating between the subgroups described by Boder (1971, 1973).

Behavioral/Affective

One of the most common results of closed head injury in children is diminished capacity and behavior problems (Hynd, Willis, 1988). The emphasis on appraising adjustment should be proportional to the referral and in some cases it seems reasonable that only a few measures will be required. In other cases, where co-occurring parental psychopathology may accentuate problems in the child, as is often found in children with co-occurring conduct disorder and hyperactivity, extensive clinical assessment of both child and parent may be necessary. As with the other domains of appraisal noted in this chapter, it makes sense that more than one measure per domain be administered. Standardized psychiatric interview schedules are particularly appealing in this regard since they typically cover most childhood psychiatric disorders. Coupled with a parent and teacher interview, a behavioral rating scale completed by both parent and teacher, and a class sociometric, a more than adequate appraisal of a child's behavioral adjustment would result.

CONCLUSIONS

This relatively brief overview of potentially meaningful measures of sensation, perception, motor, psycholinguistic, cognitive-intellectual, and behavioral development was intended to orient the reader in viewing assessment techniques from an eclectic neuropsychological perspective. More detailed descriptions of appropriate neuropsychological procedures exist elsewhere (Hynd & Obrzut, 1981; Lezak, 1976; Tramontana & Hooper, 1988). It is only through a well-thought-out analysis and assessment of a child's abilities at all levels of this information processing hierarchy that a reasonably clear picture will emerge. It bears repeating that a neuropsychological assessment should be comprehensive yet focus on the issues addressed in the referral, as briefly as possible under the circumstances, and be competently done by someone familiar with the wide array of possible measures suggested here. Even if one should chose to employ a standardized battery, it would need to be augmented with appropriate behavioral measures of adjustment and adaptive behavior.

This book has provided a perspective on how clinical neuropsychology emerged as a distinct area of specialization and has broadly discussed brain-behavior relationships and the most common procedures for their appraisal. For the clinical child psychologist to be successful in providing competent services, he must have appropriate training and supervised experience, a thorough understanding of neurophysiology and child development, a familiarization with appropriate assessment practices and procedures, and a sensitivity to the dynamic interaction between the environment, neurological status, and the child's social and emotional development.

With regard to the future, it is a reasonable expectation that an evolution may take place in the expectations of those who request and those who provide clinical child neuropsychological evaluations. As the boundaries that currently distinguish the behavioral, neurological, and psychiatric disciplines merge at certain points, an interaction must take place in developing an appreciation of what each perspective can contribute in comprehending the complexities of human behavior.

It is likely that those whose training is primarily medical in orientation will expect increased levels of expertise from psychologists in functional neuroanatomy and behavioral neurology and, therefore, very sophisticated and insightful neuropsychological evaluations. In this context it becomes increasingly evident that psychologists must become more familiar with ancillary neurodiagnostic procedures which may contribute to neuropsychological diagnosis. We have underscored this point elsewhere and forsee more involvement by psychologists in employing the results of other neurodiagnostic procedures (electrophysiological, CT, etc.) in providing an integrated perspective on brain-behavior relations in children and adolescents (Hynd & Willis, 1988). Such expectations demand that psychologists be responsible in seeking more intensive and appropriate educational experiences. Conversely, there should be an expectation by psychologists that those whose training is less behavioral and more medical should develop an appreciation of our expertise that can be offered in helping those who suffer neurological or neuropsychiatric disorders. Such expectations are indeed being met in some settings.

Thus, there is a bright future for those wishing to pursue advanced training and expertise in clinical child neuropsychology. Consistent with the points emphasized in the preface, all of us may participate in the evolving history of man's developing understanding of the human brain and behavior.

APPENDIXES

APPENDIX A: Chronology of Studies Employing the Halstead-Reitan Children's Neuropsychological Batteries or Measures Since 1945

Author(s)	N	Population	Sex	Matched	Age Range	Tests Employed	Type of Study	General Findings
			Subject Variables					
Reed, Reitan, & Klove (1965)	100	Normals (50) Brain damaged (50)	NA	Age	10–14	Wechsler-Bellevue, Finger Oscillation, Halstead Time Sense, Seashore Rhythm, Trail Making, Category, Halstead Speech-Sounds Perception, Halstead Tactual Performance	Differential diagnosis	F.S.IQ: Normal = 83–123 ($\overline{X}$ - 106) B.D. = 35–126 ($\overline{X}$ = 84) B.D. < Normals, all variables. Generally, B.D. more frequently impaired on language tests than others.
Knights & Ogilvie (1967)	212	Normals (106) Brain damaged (106)	M=55 F=51 M=77 F=29	IQ	6–14	TPT, Tapping Speed, Target Test, Auditory Closure, Sentence Memory, Verbal Fluency, Dynamcter, Category, Trail Making, Progressive Figures, Matching Pictures, Maze, Holes and Pegboard	Differential diagnosis	Best discriminators were motor or performance tasks.
Crockett, Klonoff, & Bjerring (1969)	240	Normals	M=132 F=108	—	5–8	Reitan Battery, WISC, Benton's Tests	Factor analysis	9 factors with eigenvalues over 1.0 (58.2% variance) *Factor I* (15%), Factor II (8.3%) *Factor 1* = visual-motor and analytic-synthetic skills. *Factor 2* = motor speed.
Spreen & Gaddes (1969)	Range 5–91 per age/ test	Normals	Range 4–45 (either sex)	No	6–15	Category, Finger Tapping, Speech Perception, Tactual Performance, Trail Making	Normative	Norms for age x test.

Appendix A contd.

Author(s)	N	Population	Sex	Matched	Age Range	Tests Employed	Type of Study	General Findings
				Subject Variables				
Reitan (1971a)	58	Normals (29) Brain damaged (29)	M=11 F=18 M=11 F=18	Sex and age	5–8	Finger Tapping, Grip Strength, Marching Test, Tactile Performance Test	Differential diagnosis	Motor functions: 66% hit rate Tactile-perceptual functions: 75% hit rate Time for name writing: 80% hit rate
Reitan (1971b)	98	Normals	M=51 F=47	NA	9–14	Trail Making A & B	Differential performance	No sex differences. Significant age effect. Older = better. Both A & B discriminated brain damaged from normals
	70	Normals (35) Brain damaged (35)	NA	Race, sex, age		Trail Making A & B	Differential diagnosis	
Rourke & Telegdy (1971)	45	LD (3 groups) (1) High performance-Low verbal (2)VIQ = PIQ (3) High VIQ-Low PIQ	M=45 F=0	Age and FSIQ	9–14	Smedley Hand Dynamometer, Maze Test (Kløve), Graduated Holes (Kløve), Grooved Pegboard, Finger Tapping, Tactual Performance	Differential diagnosis	Best separation of 3 groups on pegboard. No right-left hand differences effect.
Boll (1972)	54	Normals (27) Brain damaged (27)	M=16 F=11	Sex and age	NA	Category, WISC (Block Design, Reitan-Kløve Tactile Form Recognition, Seashore Rhythm, Finger Oscillation	Differential diagnosis	Sensitive to B.D.: Category > Block Design, Rhythm, Tactile Recog., Tapping.

Study	N	Groups	M/F	Variables controlled	Age range	Tests	Purpose	Findings/Conclusions
Boll & Reitan (1972a)	54	Normals (27) Brain damaged (27)	M=32 F=22	Sex, age, race	NA	Wechsler Bellevue, Halstead Neurological Test Battery for Children, Grip Strength	Identify differential test patterns	On the Halstead—B.D. < N Conclude: Different patterns for B.D. & N groups.
Boll & Reitan (1972b)	70	Normals (35) Brain damaged (35)	M=46 F=24	Race, sex, age	NA	Tactile Performance, Finger Oscillation, Grip Strength, Finger Localization, Finger-Tip Number-Writing, Tactile Form Recognition	Differential performance according to group	B.D. < N on all but Tactile Form Recognition B.D. < N dominant vs. non-dominant hand.
Boll & Reitan (1972c)	54	Normals (27) Brain damaged (27)	M=32 F=22	Race, sex, age	NA	Wechsler Bellevue, Trail Making	Differential performance according to group	B.D. = all but P.C. and Comp. correlated with Trails A. All but Obj. As. correlated with Trails B. Normal = Only Inf., D.S. correlated with Trails A and D.S. correlated with Trails B.
Reitan & Boll (1973)	94	Normals (25) Brain damaged (25) Learning disabled (25) Behavior-disordered (19)	M=56 F=38	Age	NA	WISC, Reitan-Indiana Battery, Halstead-Wepman Aphasia Test, WRAT, Finger Tapping, Grip Strength, Tactile Form Recognition, Finger Localization	Differential performance	Generally normals > behavior-problem > learning-disabled > brain-damaged children on most measures. Children with behavior problems and academic deficits perform similarly on many neuropsychological measures.
Klonoff & Low (1974)	884	Normals, Acute = head injury, Chronic = encephalopathies, M.B.D.	M > F each group	Age, sex	2–15	WISC or Stanford Binet, Reitan-Indiana, Kløve Motor Steadiness Battery, EEG	Discriminant validity (1 yr. re-eval.)	*Normals:* No sex effect. IQ related to 33/78 of variables. *Clinicals:* IQ < normals. *Chronic and Acute:* Most impaired when IQ covaried, discriminant ability greatly reduced. Discriminant analysis (neuropsychological). Initial (76–85%) Re-evaluation (73–96%) hit rate.

Author(s)	N	Subject Variables					Tests Employed	Type of Study	General Findings
		Population	Sex	Matched	Age Range				
Reitan (1974)	58	Normal (29) Brain damaged (29)	M=11 F=18 M=11 F=18	Sex, age	5–8		WISC, WRAT, Reitan-Indiana Neuropsychological Test Battery	Differential diagnosis	Significant differences on all variables except grip strength. F.S. IQ best discriminator. Verbal and visual-spatial sequential more impaired than incidental memory.
Rourke & Finlayson (1975)	45	Low academics (3 groups): 1. Normal Trails A & B 2. Normal A. impaired B 3. Impaired A & B	NA	Age & IQ	10–14		Trail Making A & B, WISC, PPVT, Sentence Memory, Verbal Fluency, Aphasia Screening, Target Category, Grooved Pegboard	Differential pattern performance of Trails groups	Differences found on IQ measures. 1 > 3 – Pegboard. No difference on Category Test. Group 2 = deficits in left hemisphere; 3 = deficits in right hemisphere.
Finlayson: Reitan (1976a)	120	Normals (20 at each age level)	M & F	F.S. IQ age, education	6–14 (6, 7, 8, 12, 13, 14 age levels)		Finger Tapping, Grip Strength, Tactile Finger Localization, Finger-Tip Symbol Recognition	Normative	Right > left for motor functions but not tactile-perceptual (all ages).
Finlayson & Reitan (1976b)	201	Older normal Younger normal	Older: M=15 F=9 Younger: M=10 F=10	No	Older: 12–14 Younger: 6–8		WISC, WRAT, Category Test, Tactile Imperception, Tactile Finger Recognition, Finger Tip Writing Perception, Tactile Form Recognition	Differential performance by tactile, perceptual error groups	*Good tactile groups:* *Older*=higher Category, Reading, V.IQ and F.S.IQ. No difference P.IQ *Younger*=higher V.IQ and F.S.IQ.

Study	N	Sample		Variables controlled	Age	Tests	Purpose	Results
Tsushima & Towne (1977)	62	Learning problems (31) Questionable brain damage (31)	Each group M=28 F=3	Age, sex, SES, handedness	6–8	WISC, WRAT, Reitan-Indiana Neuropsychological Test Battery	Differential diagnosis	No difference on Category, P.IQ, Reading. QBD < N on all variables except WISC arithmetic. 10/37 variables significant (.05) Discriminant analysis: Hit rate (5 variables) 72% Hit rate (Battery) 85%
Rourke & Finlayson (1978)	45	Learning and/or perception problems 1. Read, spell, math=2+ years below (15) 2. Read, spell=1.8+ years < math (15) 3. Read, spell=2+ years > math	M=13 F=2 M=15 F=0 M=11 F=4	Age & IQ	9–14	WRAT, WISC—R, PPVT, Aphasia Screening, Halstead Speech-Sounds, Auditory Closure, Sentence Memory, Target	Differential diagnosis (patterns)	Group 3 > 2 all 10 measures (V.IQ > P.IQ) 1 & 2 similar (1=V.IQ>P.IQ) 1 > 3 (verbal-auditory) 1 < 3 (visual-spatial)
Townes, Reitan, & Trupin (1978)	54	Normal (27) Brain damaged (27)	M=18 F=36	Sex and age	NA	WISC, Category, Matching Pictures	Correlational and differential diagnosis	IQ: N > B.D. B.D.=significant correlation of IQ with Category and Matching Pictures. Normals=No correlation.

Appendix A *contd.*

Author(s)	N	Subject Variables				Tests Employed	Type of Study	General Findings
		Population	Sex	Matched	Age Range			
Selz & Reitan (1979a)	75	Normal (25) LD (25) Brain damaged (25)	M=15 F=10 M=19 F=6 M=15 F=10	NA	9–14	Halstead Neurological Test Battery for Children, Trail Making, Reitan-Kløve Sensory Perception Examination, Strength of Grip, Reitan-Indiana Aphasia Screening, Wechsler-Bellevue or WISC	Differential diagnosis	Application of 37 rules from pilot study. Hit rate = 73%
Selz & Reitan (1979b)	75	Normal (25) LD = (25) Brain damaged (25)	M=15 F=10 M=19 F= 6 M=15 F=10	NA	9–14	Halstead Neurological Test Battery for Children, Trail Making, WISC or Wechsler-Bellevue	Differential diagnosis	No age effect. 11 of 13 psychological measures differed. N > LD > BD = Trail A. P.IQ, F.S. IQ N > LD & BD = Category, Speech, Rhythm, & V.IQ. N & LD > BD = TPT (time) Trails B, tapping. Hit rate = 80%.
Townes et al. (1980)	456	Normals	M=239 F=217	No	5–9	WISC, Reitan-Indiana, Stanford Early School Achievement Test, Stanford Achievement Test	Differential performance	Neuropsychological variables predicted academic achievement = 50%. 10 best neuropsychological or IQ identified 75% S's achievement.
Dunleavy, Hansen, & Baade (1981)	24	Asthmatic (7) Control (17)	M=13 F=11	NA	9–14	Halstead Neuropsychological Test Battery, WISC, Lateral Dominance Examination, Category, Trail Making, TPT, Seashore	Differential performance	Halstead tests measuring performance skills were more sensitive to neuropsychological impairment than Halstead tests

	N	Groups	Sex		Age	Rhythm, Speech-Sounds Perception, Tactile Form Recognition, Finger Tapping, Grip Strength, Aphasia Screening		measuring verbal or language related skills.
Klegas & Fisher (1981)	64	Normal (35) Brain damaged (29)	M=23 F=12 M=21 F=8	No	5–14	WISC—R, Reitan-Indiana Neurological Test Battery for Children, Children's Assessment of Cerebral Dysfunction (CACD)	Differential diagnosis; CAT scan vs. multiple soft signs	CAT scan, CACD, and F.S.IQ best correlates (5–14 years). Hit rate = 88–90%. Soft signs criterion 5–8 years: Obj. As. Coding and D. Sy. Hit rate = 78%. 9–14 years: CACD and V. IQ. Hit rate = 76%
Daugherty & Moran (1982)	51	Legally blind (21) Low vision (30)	M=63% F=37%	No	7–18	Category, TPT Finger Oscillation, Rhythm, Speech-Sounds, Aphasia, WRAT, Marching Test, Color Forms and Progressive Figures, Target Test, Bender, Stephens Piagetian Battery of Reasoning Assessment, WISC—R or WAIS	Differential performance according to group: factor analysis	*V.IQ:* Blind=97, Low vision=91 *P.IQ:* Blind=80, Low vision=89 *F.S.IQ:* Blind=88, Low vision=89 *9–14:* Motor/visual impairment correlated with neuropsychological functioning.
Wolf & Tramontana (1982)	35	Hospitalized psychiatric patients	M=25 F=10	No	9–15	Reitan-Indiana Aphasia, Halstead Neurological Test Battery for Children, Reitan-Kløve Sensory-Perceptual Examination, Trail Making, Strength of Grip, WISC—R	Correlational	*Aphasia Categories:* Spelling dyspraxia (77%) Construct dyspraxia (57%) Dyslexia (60%) Central dysarthria (66%) Dyscalculia (63%) Right-Left Confusion (51%) Aphasia Test correlated with total battery (.69)

Appendix A contd.

Author(s)	N	Subject Variables				Tests Employed	Type of Study	General Findings
		Population	Sex	Matched	Age Range			
Dean (1983)	61	Epileptics (major motor)	M=48 F=13	No	10–14	WISC—R, Trail Making, Category, Finger Oscillation, Tactile Performance, Speech-Sounds	Correlational; compared to normal population	Severe abstract reasoning deficits; rather global impairment characterized epileptic patients
Incagnoli & Kane (1983)	13	Gilles de la Tourette Syndrome	M	NA	10–13	WISC—R, WRAT, Halstead Neurological Battery for Children, Bender Gestalt	Normative for syndrome	$WISC—R$ (means): F.S. IQ=96, V.IQ=97, P.IQ=97 Coding significantly low ($\bar{X}=5.9$) $WRAT$ (means): Read=106, Spell=99, Math=81 (2 yr. < CA) $Halstead$: normal=11; LD=1; B.D.=1, Bender=16 months < CA.
Klegas (1983)	64	5–8 yr. Normals (11) Brain damaged (11) 9–14 yr. Normals (24) Brain damaged (18)	M=6 F=5 M=8 F=3 M=17 F=7 M=13 F=5	NA	5–8 yr. 9–14 yr	WISC—R, Children's Assessment of Cerebral Dysfunction, Reitan-Indiana or Halstead Neurological Test for Children	Correlational	5–8 yr. sample: Category, Progressive Figures, Color Form correlated with V., P., F.S.IQ 9–14 yr. sample: All but Tapping and Rhythm correlated with IQ
Obrzut, Hynd & Obrzut (1983)	46	Normals LD	M=32 F=14	Sex, age, sociocultural environment	9–13	WISC—R, TPT, Category Test, Edinburgh Handedness Inventory, Dichotic Listening Test (directed attention conditions)	Differential diagnosis	Hit rate=95.6% Directed dichotic listening task and V.IQ best discriminators between groups

Study	N	Group	Sex	Matching	Age	Tests	Purpose	Results
O'Leary et al. (1983)	106	Epileptic patients	NA	No	9–15	WISC—R, Categories, TPT, Trails A & B, Tonal Memory, Rhythm, Speech, Grip, Tapping	Differential effects of age onset of epilepsy	No age of onset and diagnosis effect.
Seidenberg, Giordani, Berent, & Boll (1983)	121	Seizure disorder	M=62 F=59	Age, age of seizure onset, sex	9–14	Halstead-Reitan Neuropsychological Test Battery. WISC—R	Difference of IQ on Battery; right-left hand difference in performance	6 of 14 measures (H-R) = IQ influence at IQ < 80 and > 100 only. Left hand = right hand on basic motor tasks.
Tecter (1983)	105	Normals	M=52 F=53	No	4-11 to 6-7	McCarthy Test, Aphasia Screening, Matching Pictures, Finger Tapping, Progressive Figures, Color Form, Target, Matching Figure, Matching vs. Tactile, Imperception, Star and Concentric Squares	Comparison of IQ measures to Neuropsychological	Canonical analysis = all variables Verbal comp. & perception perf. correlated with Aphasia Total Error. 5 factors found.
Camfield, Gates, (Exp.1) Ronen, Camfield, Ferguson, & MacDonald (1984)	27	Pure left (13) or right (14) temporal lobe epilepsy (TLE)	M=15 (7L, 8R) F=12 (6L, 6R)	Sex, age, grade No. seizures	6–17	WISC—R or WAIS, PPVT, Trails A and B, Category, TPT, Sentence Repetition Test, Rosner Auditory Analysis Test, Finger Tap, PIC, Grooved Pegboard	Differential diagnosis	No significant differences between left and right TLE groups on tests of intelligence, achievement, and neuropsychological. PIC; except WRAT math.
Camfield et al. (cont.) (Exp. 2)	27	Maladjusted (10) Good adjustment (17)	NA	NA	NA	Same as in Exp. 1.	Differential diagnosis	Maladjusted < adjusted on V.IQ, P.IQ, F.S.IQ, WRAT (Spell, Math), PPVT, and most other variables.

Appendix A contd.

Author(s)	N	Subject Variables			Age Range	Tests Employed	Type of Study	General Findings
		Population	Sex	Matched				
Gulbrandsen (1984)	112	Normals Concussion (C)	M=38 F=18 M=38 F=18	Sex, grade, academic achievement	9–13	Category, TPT, Trails, Finger Tapping, Halstead-Wepman Screening for Aphasia, Seashore Rhythm, Stereognosis, Grooved Pegboard, WISC	Differential performance	C < N on 29 of 32 variables, (none at 13 years). Concluded that Neuropsychological deficits with normal school functioning characterize children with concussion.
Winogran, Knights, & Bawden (1984)	51	Mild injury (17) Moderate injury (17) Severe injury (17)	M=30 F=21	Sex, age at injury and testing	4.7–17.6	WISC—R, PPVT, WRAT, Category, TPT, Tapping, Finger Agnosia, Pegboard, Aphasia Screening, Sensory Memory, Fluency, Target, Trails	Retrospective study comparing 3 groups	Profiles: Mild and Severe least similar. Severe pattern most distinctive.
Teeter (1985)	105	Normals	M=52 F=53	NA	Mean age =5–6	McCarthy Scales of Children's Abilities, Aphasia Screening Test, Matching Pictures, Progressive Figures, Target Test, Color Form, Tapping	Longitudinal (2 years) predictive validity	McCarthy and Reitan tasks similar in accuracy in discriminating high, average, and low readers. Predictor variables stable across two years.
Strom, Gray, Dean, & Fischer (1987)	989	Referred for LD evaluation	M=738 F=251	NA	9–14 Mean age =11.4	WISC—R, WRAT, Halstead-Reitan Neuropsychological Battery	Predictive validity	A significant increase (16–30%) in predictive ability found over WISC—R scores using Halstead-Reitan tests in relation to WRAT performance.

Note: Other recent studies employing these test batteries or measures have focused less on issues related to validity (i.e., content, discriminate or predictive); rather, they have employed the tests to examine clinical or theoretical issues. The studies cited in this Appendix are most frequently cited as sources establishing the validity of these measures.

Abbreviations: B.D. (Brain damaged), C (Concussion), CA (Chronological Age), CACD (Children's Assessment of Cerebral Dysfunction), CAT (Computerized Axial Tomography), Comp. (Comprehension Subtest on WISC), D.S. (Digit Span Subtest), D.Sy. (Digit Symbol Subtest), EEG (Electroencephalography), F (Female), F.S.IQ (Full Scale IQ, Inf. (Information Subtest), LD (Learning-Disabled), M (Male), NA (Not Available), N (Normal), Obj. As. (Object Assembly Subtest), P.C. (Picture Completion), PIC (Personality Inventory for Children), P.IQ (Performance IQ), PPVT (Peabody Picture Vocabulary Test), QBD (Questionable Brain Damage), TLE (Temporal Lobe Epilepsy), TPT (Tactual Performance Test), V.IQ (Verbal IQ), WAIS (Wechsler Adult Intelligence Scale), WISC/WISC-R (Wechsler Intelligence Scale for Children-Revised), WRAT (Wide Range Achievement Test).

119

APPENDIX B: Chronology of Studies Employing the Luria-Nebraska Neuropsychological Battery—Children's Revision (LNNB—CR)

Author(s)	N	Subject Variables Population	Subject Variables Sex	Subject Variables Matched	Age Range	Tests Employed	Type of Study	General Findings
Wilkening, Golden, MacInnes, Plaisted, & Hermann (1981)	201	Normal (125) & Brain damaged (76)	NA	No	NA	LNNB—CR	Validation of LNNB—CR. Differentiating BD from normals.	86.2% hit rate in correctly classifying subjects into groups.
Gustavson, Golden, Leark, Wilkening, Hermann, & Plaisted (1982)	350	Normal & Brain damaged	NA	No	NA	LNNB—CR, WISC—R WRAT	Correlational IQ as covariates	Correlations LNNB—CR: F.S. IQ (.86). V. IQ (.83): P. IQ (.83); Math (.73); Read (.87); Spell (.81). On 8 of all 11 scales BD differentiated from normals (except IQ process, reading, and tactile).
Gustavson, Wilkening, Hermann, & Plaisted (1982)	201	See Wilkening et al., 1981	NA	No	NA	LNNB—CR	Cluster analysis	34 factors with wide range of variability in number of factors/scale. Maximum = 9 on motor scale; minimum 1 factor on arithmetic and reading (each).
Hermann (1982a)	50	Epileptic	NA	NA	NA	LNNB—CR, Child Behavior Profile	—	Poor performance on LNNB—CR associated with poor school performance and poor social competence.

Appendix B *contd.*

Author(s)	N	Subject Variables Population	Sex	Matched	Age Range	Tests Employed	Type of Study	General Findings
Hermann (1982b)	66	Epileptic	NA	NA	NA	LNNB—CR, Child Behavior Profile	Neuropsychological correlates of aggression	LNNB—CR discriminates between aggressive and non-aggressive. Deficits in verbal abilities as measured by 7 different scales.
Leark, Gustavson, Wilkening, & Golden (1982)	NA	NA	NA	NA	NA	LNNB—CR, WISC—R	Can scales predict WISC—R scores	Predicted 4 groups: IQ ≥ 116, IQ=85–115 IQ=70–84, IQ < 70 (70% accuracy). Higher IQ: weakest Lower IQ: best
Sherrets, Quattrocchi, & Menolascino (1982)	1	Supravalvular aortic stenosis (William's Syndrome)	M	No	8 yr. 1 mo.	WISC—R, LNNB—CR, WRAT, PIAT, PPVT, Child Behavior Profile (Achenbach), Developmental Profile II	Case study	Verbal IQ=45; performance IQ=40; FSIQ=40; PPVT IQ=74 WRAT (SS): Spelling=46. Reading=61, Math=63. PIAT (SS): 65–77 range LNNB—CR: all scores > 80.
Carr (1983)	55	Psychiatric (32) Brain damaged (23)	M=30 F=25	No	8–12	LNNB—CR, WISC—R	Discriminate validity. Compare LNNB—CR with WISC—R.	Significant age effect for LNNB—CR. Significant diagnosis on LNNB—CR & WISC—R ($p < .001$) & for each subtest of both. LNNB—CR=82% correct

classification rate. WISC—R=85% correct classification rate.

Study	N	Groups	Gender	Covariate	Age	Tests	Purpose	Results
Carr, Sweet, Rossini, & Angara (1983)	96	Normal (32) Psychiatric (32) Neurological Impaired (32)	M=48 F=48	No	8–12	WISC—R, LNNB—CR	Cross-validational discriminant ability	Normal > psychiatric > neurologically impaired in test performance. However, when IQ entered as a covariate, the effect disappeared. LNNB—CR correct classification=84% for psychiatric, 78% neurological. WISC—R correct classification=78% psychiatric, 91% neurological.
Hyman (1983)	60	LD (30) Non-disabled (30)	NA	NA	10–11	LNNB—CR	Differential diagnoses	LNNB—CR discriminated groups. LD=4 subscales > 60. Conclusions LD performed normally on basic sensory, motor, and simple linguistic skills but dificient in complex multimodal sensory and language processing.
Nolan, Hammeke, & Barkley (1983)	36	a. Normal WRAT ≥ 40 percentile; b. Read-Spell ≤ 20 percentile Math ≥ 40; c. Math ≤ 20 percentile read-spell ≥ 40	9M 3F; 10M 2F; 9M 3F	No	7–13	WISC—R, FTNW, Finger, Agnosia, LNNB—CR, WRAT	Determine whether LD subtypes would exhibit unique neuropsychological profiles.	Normal > group b on expressive language, writing, and reading. No significant difference between normals and group c. Group b had lower scores on Verbal IQ and linguistic tasks of LNNB—CR (expressive speech, writing, and reading).

Appendix B contd.

Author(s)	N	Subject Variables				Tests Employed	Type of Study	General Findings
		Population	Sex	Matched	Age Range			
Quattrocchi & Golden (1983)	86	Normal	M=31 F=55	No	8–13	PPVT—R, LNNB—CR	Correlation between tests	Significant small r = PPVT–R and LNNB—CR ($\leq = .05$). Visual= –.26, perception = –.38, arithmetic = –.32, memory = –.25, intelligence = –.41.
Snow, Hartlage, Hynd, & Grant (1983)	40	LD	34M 6F	No	8–12	LNNB—CR, MPD	Construct validity	MPD not correlated with LNNB—CR (MPD corrected for IQ while LNNB—CR is not. LNNB—CR results may reflect effect of "g".)
Snyder, Leark, Golden, Grove, Allison (1983)	46	LD	NA	No	8–12	WISC—R, LNNB—CR, K-ABC	Correlational	Correlations of IQ measures and LNNB—CR scales. LNNB—CR scales to K-ABC—(range –.01 to –.64). Motor and intellectual processes correlated with all but K-ABC Achievement scale. Conclusion—LNNB—CR measures a significant construct of intelligence.
Geary & Gilger (1984)	34	Normal (17) LD (17)	M=9 F=8 M=11 F=6	Mean age, grade, V&P IQ	8–13	LNNB—CR, WISC—R	Differential performance of N & LD	Significant difference 4 scales. Normals > LD Rhythm, expressive language, writing, and reading.

Study	N	Groups	Sex	Matching variables	Age	Tests	Purpose	Findings
Geary, Jennings, Schultz, & Alper (1984)	30	Normal (15) / LD (15)	M=9 F=6 / M=9 F=6	Age, grade placement, sex	9-12	LNNB–CR, WISC–R	Differential diagnosis accuracy	93.3% accuracy rate of diagnosis (all LD's diagnosed LD, only 2 normals diagnosed LD).
Gustavson, (Exp. 1) Golden, Wilkening, Hermann, Plaisted, MacInnes, & Leark (1984)	125	Normal (IQ > 80)	60M 65F	No	8-12 (25 at each year level)	LNNB–CR, WISC–R, WRAT	Normative. Establish critical level formula.	Scoring system (0, 1, 2) developed to eliminate age differences. Norms established.
(Exp. 2)	149	Normal (91) (IQ > 82) / Brain injured (58)	47M 44F / 28M 30F	Demographic variables	B-D ($\bar{X}$ = 10.46)	LNNB–CR, WISC–R, WRAT, PPVT	Validation of norm reference & critical level formula.	CL (critical level) = 82.02 – (.14 × age in months).
Sawicki, Leark, Golden, & Karras (1984) (a) derivation study	201	Normal =125) / Brain injured (76)	NA	Age, gender, education	8-12	LNNB-CR	Development of additional clinical scales.	3 new scales developed. (a) Pathognomonic scale = 13 items; (b) Left sensorimotor scale = 9 items; (c) right sensorimotor scale = 9 items. All three scales significant p < .001.
(b) cross-validation study	149	Normal (91) / Brain injured (58)	NA	No	8-12	LNNB–CR	Cross-validation of scales.	Internal consistency derivation group P = .86, L = .82, R = .81; cross-validation group P = .88, L = .83, R = .81. Cross-validation = 89.3%.
Snow, Hynd, & Hartlage (1984)	40	LD	18M 2F	No	8-12	WISC-R, WRAT, LNNB-CR	Differential diagnosis 2 LD groups (mild/severe)	Significant (P <.01) difference on 4 of 11 scales of LNNB–CR with severe LD—more impairment (receptive, writing, reading, arithmetic).

Appendix B contd.

Author(s)	N	Subject Variables Population	Sex	Matched	Age Range	Tests Employed	Type of Study	General Findings
Gilger & Geary (1985)	56	LD	35M 22F	Age & F.S.IQ	8–13	LNNB—CR	Sensitivity of LNNB—CR to verbal & nonverbal cognitive deficits.	LNNB—CR seems differentially sensitive to verbal & nonverbal deficits. Receptive speech scale reliably sensitive to V. IQ deficiencies, & no subscale reliably sensitive to P.IQ deficits.
McKay, Sterling, Baumann, Car, Walsh, & Gilmore (1985)	1	Removal carniopharyngioma	F	NA	11 years	LNNB—CR	Case study involving patient with frontal lobe dysfunction.	Conclusions—LNNB—CR is sensitive to frontal lobe signs if quantitative item analysis is supplemented with qualitative observation.
Snow & Hynd (1985)	100	LD	85M 15F	No	8–12	LNNB—CR, WISC—R, WRAT	Differential diagnosis of LD subtypes.	72% subjects classified into distinct subgroups, but all 3 groups probably represent variation of language disordered LD.
Snow & Hynd (1985)	100	LD	85M 15F	No	8–12	LNNB—CR	Factor structure	3 factors (64% of variance)—scales of LNNB—CR 1. Visual, receptive, expressive, arithmetic, memory, intelligence. 2. Writing and reading. 3. Motor, rhythm, & tactile.

| Karras, Newlin, Franzen, Golden, Wilkening, Rothermel, & Tramontana (1987) | 719 | Normal (240) Brain damaged (253) Suspected brain damaged (32) LD (39) Leukemic (5) Psychiatric (150) | No | M = 406 F = 313 | 8–12 | LNNB—CR | Factor analysis | 11 factors found. Factor 1 measures basic academic skills, Factor 2 spatial-directional abilities, and Factor 3 spatially based movement. |

Abbreviations: BD (Brain Damaged), CL (Critical Level), F (Female), F.S.IQ (Full Scale IQ), FTNW (Finger-Tip Number Writing), K-ABC (Kaufman Assessment Battery for Children), LD (Learning-Disabled), M (Male), MPD (Minnesota Percepto-Diagnostic Test), N (Normal), NA (Not Available), PIAT (Peabody Individual Achievement Test), P.IQ (Performance IQ), PPVT/PPVT—R (Peabody Picture Vocabulary Test—Revised), SS (Standard Score), V.IQ (Verbal IQ), WISC—R (Wechsler Intelligence Scale for Children—Revised), WRAT (Wide Range Achievement Test).

REFERENCES

Aaron, P. G. (1981). Diagnosis and remediation of learning disabilities in children—A neuropsychological key approach. In G. W. Hynd & J. E. Obrzut (Eds.), *Neuropsychological assessment and the school-age child: Issues and procedures* (pp. 303–333). New York: Grune & Stratton, Inc.

Alajouanine, T. H., & Lhermitte, F. (1965). Acquired aphasia in children. *Brain, 88,* 653–662.

April, R. S., & Han, M. (1980). Crossed aphasia in a right-handed bilingual Chinese man. *Archives of Neurology, 37,* 342–346.

Bailey, P. (1970). Pierre Marie. In W. Haymaker & F. Schiller (Eds.), *The founders of neurology* (2nd ed., pp. 476–479). Springfield, IL: Charles C Thomas, Publishers.

Bailey, P., & Bonin, C. Von (1951). *The isocortex of man.* Urbana, IL: The University of Illinois Press.

Bakker, D. J. (1981). Cognitive deficits and cerebral asymmetry. *Journal of Research and Development in Education, 15,* 48–54.

Bannatyne, A. D. (1971). *Language, reading and learning disabilities.* Springfield: Charles C Thomas.

Bannatyne, A. (1974). Diagnosis: A note on recategorization of the WISC scaled scores. *Journal of Learning Disabilities, 7,* 272–274.

Bastian, H. C. (1898). *Aphasia and other speech defects.* London: H. K. Lewis.

Becker, M. G., Isaac, W., & Hynd, G. W. (1988). Neuropsychological development of non-verbal behaviors attributed to "frontal lobe" functioning. *Developmental Neuropsychology* (in press).

Benton, A. L. (1955). Right-left discrimination and finger localization in defective children. *Archives of Neurology and Psychiatry, 74,* 583–589.

Benton, A. L. (1959). *Right-left discrimination and finger localization: Development and pathology.* New York: Hoeber.

Benton, A. L. (1974). Hemispheric dominance before Broca. *Neuropsychologia, 22,* 807–811.

Benton, A. L., Hamsher, K., Varney, N. R., & Spreen, O. (1983). *Contributions to neuropsychological assessment: A clinical manual.* New York: Oxford University Press.

Benton, A. L., & Joynt, R. J. (1960). Early descriptions of aphasia. *Archives of Neurology, 3,* 205–222.

Berg, R. A., Bolter, J. F., Ch'ien, L. T., Williams, S. J., Lancaster, W., & Cummins, J. (1984). Comparative diagnostic accuracy of the Halstead-Reitan & the Luria-Nebraska Neuropsychological Adults & Children's Batteries. *Clinical Neuropsychology, 6,* 200–204.

Beery, K. E. (1974). *Developmental Test of Visual-Motor Integration.* New York: Psychological Corporation.

Bieliauskas, L., & Boll, T. (1984). Division 40/INS Task Force on Education, Accreditation & Credentialing. *APA Newsletter 40.*

Bigelow, H. J. (1850). *Dr. Harlow's case of recovery from the passage of an iron bar through the head.* (Cited in Weinstein, 1984).

Bigler, E. D. (1987). Acquired cerebral trauma: Epidemiology, neuropsychological assessment and academic/educational deficits. *Journal of Learning Disabilities, 20,* 516–517.

Boder, E. (1971). Developmental dyslexia: Prevailing diagnostic concepts and a new diagnostic approach. In H. Myklebust (Ed.), *Progress in learning disabilities.* New York: Grune & Stratton, Inc.

Boder, E. (1973). Developmental dyslexia: A diagnostic approach based on three atypical reading patterns. *Developmental Medicine and Child Neurology, 15,* 663–687.

Bogen, J. E. (1969). The other side of the brain: Part I. *Bulletin of the Los Angeles Neurological Society, 34,* 73–105.

Bogen, J. E. (1975). Some educational aspects of hemispheric specialization. *U.C.L.A. Educator, 17,* 24–32.

Boll, T. J. (1972). Conceptual vs. perceptual vs. motor deficits in brain-damaged children. *Journal of Clinical Psychology, 28,* 157–159.

Boll, T. J. (1974). Behavioral correlates of cerebral damage in children aged 9 through 14. In R. M. Reitan & L. A. Davison (Eds.), *Clinical neuropsychology: Current status and applications* (pp. 91–120). Washington, DC: V. H. Winston & Sons.

Boll, T. J., & Barth, J. T. (1981). Neuropsychology of brain damage in children. In S. B. Filshov & J. B. Boll (Eds.), *Handbook of clinical neuropsychology* (pp. 418–452). New York: John Wiley & Sons.

Boll, T. J., & Reitan, R. M. (1972a). Comparative ability interrelationships in normal & brain-damaged children. *Journal of Clinical Psychology, 28,* 152–156.

Boll, T. J., & Reitan, R. M. (1972b). Motor and tactile-perceptual deficits in brain-damaged children. *Perceptual and Motor Skills, 34,* 343–350.

Boll, T. J., & Reitan, R. M. (1972c). The comparative intercorrelations of brain-damaged and normal children on the Trail-Making Test and the Wechsler-Bellevue Scale. *Journal of Clinical Psychology, 28,* 491–493.

Bray, P. F., Bale, J. F., Anderson, R. E., & Kern, E. R. (1981). Progressive neurological disease associated with chronic cytomegalovirus infection. *Annals of Neurology, 9,* 499–502.

Broca, P. (1861). Nouvelle observation daphemie produite par une lesion de la muite posterieure des dexième et troisième circonvolutions frontales. *Bulletin de la Society Anatomique de Paris, 36,* 398–407.

Brown-Sequard, C. E. (1877). *Dual character of the brain.* Washington, DC: Smithsonian Institute.

Burckhardt, G. (1891). Ueber Rindenexcisionen als beitrag zur operativen therapie der psychosen. *Zeitschrift fuer Psychologie, 47,* 463–548.

Camfield, P. R., Gates, R., Ronen, G., Camfield, C., Ferguson, A., & MacDonald, G. W. (1984). Comparison of cognitive ability, personality profile, and school success in epileptic children with pure right versus left temporal lobe EEG foci. *Annals of Neurology, 15,* 122–126.

Campbell, S., & Whitaker, H. (1986). Cortical maturation and developmental neurolinguistics. In J. E. Obrzut & G. W. Hynd (Eds.), *Child neuropsychology: Theory and research* (vol. 1, pp. 55–72). New York: Academic Press.

Carr, M. (1983). A test of clinical utility: The Luria-Nebraska Neuropsychological Battery, Children's Revision. (Doctoral dissertation, Boston University Graduate School, 1983). *Dissertation Abstracts International, 44,* (5-B), 1586.

Carr, M. A., Sweet, J. J., Rossini, E., Angara, V. K. (1983). Diagnostic accuracy of the Luria-Nebraska Battery—Children's Revision. Paper presented at the meeting of the American Psychological Association, Anaheim, CA.

Centofanti, C. C., & Smith, A. (1978). *The single and double simultaneous (face-hand) stimulation test*. Los Angeles: Western Psychological Service.

Chadwick, O., & Rutter, M. (1983). Neuropsychological assessment. In M. Rutter (Ed.), *Developmental neuropsychiatry* (pp. 181–212). New York: Guilford Press.

Christensen, A. -L. (1979). *Luria's neuropsychological investigation*. Munksgaard: Copenhagen.

Clarke, E., & O'Malley, C. D. (1968). *The human brain and spinal cord*. Berkeley, CA: The University of California Press.

Coles, G. S. (1978). The learning disabilities test batteries: Empirical and social issues. *Harvard Educational Review, 48*, 313–340.

Comrey, A. C. (1978). Common methodological problems in factor analytic studies. *Journal of Consulting and Clinical Psychology, 46*, 648–659.

Craig, D. L. (1979). Neuropsychological assessment in public psychiatric hospitals: The current state of practice. *Clinical Neuropsychology, 1*, 1–7.

Critchley, M. (1986). Hughlings Jackson: The man and his time. *Archives of Neurology, 43*, 435–437.

Crockett, D., Klonoff, H., Bjerring, J. (1969). Factor analysis of neuropsychological tests. *Perceptual and Motor Skills, 29*, 791–802.

Crome, L. (1960). The brain in mental retardation. *British Medical Journal, 16*, 897–904.

Damasio, A. (1984). Behavioral neurology: Research and practice. *Seminars in Neurology, 4*, 117–119.

Damasio, A. R., & Galaburda, A. M. (1985). Norman Geschwind. *Archives of Neurology, 42*, 500–504.

Daugherty, K. M., & Moran, M. F. (1982). Neuropsychological learning and developmental characteristics of the low vision child. *Visual Impairment and Blindness, 76* (10), 398–406.

Dean, R. S. (1983). Neuropsychological correlates of total seizures with major motor epileptic children. *Clinical Neuropsychology, 5* (1), 1–3.

DeMyer, W. (1974). *Technique of the neurological examination: A programmed text* (2nd ed.). New York: McGraw-Hill Book Company.

Detmold, W. (1850). Abscess in the substance of the brain: The lateral ventricle opened by an operation. *American Journal of the Medical Sciences, 1*, 86–95.

Diller, L., Ben-Yishay, Y., Gerstmann, L. J., Goodkin, R., Gordon, W., & Weinberg, J. (1974). *Studies in cognition and rehabilitation in hemiplegia*. New York: New York University Medical Center Institute of Rehabilitation.

Doehring, D. G. (1968). *Patterns of impairment in specific reading disability: A neuropsychological investigation*. Bloomington: Indiana University Press.

Downs, M. P. (1977). The expanding imperatives of early identification. In F. H. Bess (Ed.), *Childhood deafness* (pp. 95–106). New York: Grune & Stratton, Inc.

Drake, W. E. (1968). Clinical and pathological findings in a child with a developmental learning disability. *Journal of Learning Disabilities, 1*, 486–502.

Duane, D. D. (1979). Toward a definition of dyslexia: A summary of views. *Bulletin of the Orton Society, 29*, 56–64.

Duffy, F. H., Denckla, M. B., Bartels, P. H., & Sandini, L. S. (1980). Dyslexia: Automated diagnosis by computerized brain electrical activity. *Annals of Neurology, 7*, 421–428.

Dunleavy, R. A., Hansen, J. L., & Baade, L. E. (1981). Discriminating powers of Halstead Battery Tests in assessment of 9- to 14-year-old severely asthmatic children. *Clinical Neuropsychology, 3,* 9–12.

Dykman, R. A., Ackerman, P. T., Clements, S. D., & Peters, J. E. (1971). Specific learning disabilities: An attentional deficit syndrome. In H. R. Myklebust (Ed.), *Progress in learning disabilities* (vol. 2). New York: Grune & Stratton, Inc.

Dykman, R. A., Ackerman, P. T., & McCray, D. S. (1980). Effects of methylphenidate on selective and sustained attention in hyperactive, reading-disabled, and presumably attention-disordered boys. *Journal of Nervous and Mental Disease, 168,* 745–752.

Dykman, R. A., Ackerman, P. T., & Oglesby, D. M. (1979). Selective and sustained attention in hyperactive, learning-disabled, and normal boys. *Journal of Nervous and Mental Disease, 167,* 288–297.

Elbert, J. C., Culbertson, J. L., Gerrity, K. M., Guthrie, L. J., & Bayles, R. (1985). Neuropsychological and electrophysiologic follow-up of children surviving acute lymphocytic leukemia. Paper presented at the annual meeting of the International Neuropsychological Society, San Diego, February.

Ernhart, C. A., Graham, F. K., Eichman, P. C., Marshall, J. M., & Thurston, D. (1963). Brain injury in the preschool child: Some developmental considerations: II. Comparison of brain-injured and normal children. *Psychological Monographs, 77* (all of No. 573).

Ettlinger, G. (1984). Humans, apes, and monkeys: The changing neuropsychological viewpoint. *Neuropsychologia, 22,* 685–696.

Fedio, P., & Mirsky, A. F. (1969). Selective intellectual deficits in children with temporal lobe or centrencephalic epilepsy. *Neuropsychologia, 7,* 287–300.

Ferraro, A. (1970). Camillo Golgi. In W. Haymaker & F. Schiller (Eds.), *The founders of neurology* (2nd ed., pp. 35–39). Springfield, IL: Charles C Thomas, Publishers.

Fields, F.R.J., & Whitmyre, J. W. (1969). Verbal and performance relationships with respect to laterality of cerebral involvement. *Diseases of the Nervous System, 30,* 177–179.

Finlayson, M.A.J., & Reitan, R. M. (1976a). Handedness in relation to measures of motor & tactile-perceptual functions in normal children. *Perceptual & Motor Skills, 43,* 475–481.

Finlayson, M.A.J., & Reitan, R. M. (1976b). Tactile-perceptual functioning in relation to intellectual, cognitive & reading skills in younger & older normal children. *Developmental Medicine & Child Neurology, 18,* 442–446.

Freytag, E., & Lindenberg, R. (1967). Neuropathologic findings in patients of a hospital for the mentally deficient: A survey of 359 cases. *John Hopkins Medical Journal, 14,* 379–392.

Friedman, R. M., Sandler, J., Hernandez, M., & Wolfe, D. A. (1981). Child abuse. In E. J. Marsh & L. G. Terdal (Eds.), *Behavioral assessment of childhood disorders.* New York: Guilford Press.

Frisch, G. R., & Handler, L. A. (1974). A neuropsychological investigation of "functional disorders of speech articulation." *Journal of Speech and Hearing Research, 17,* 432–445.

Gaddes, W. H. (1968). Neuropsychological approach to learning disorders. *Journal of Learning Disabilities, 1,* 523–534.

Gaddes, W. H. (1969). Can educational psychology be neurological? *Canadian Journal of Behavioral Science, 1,* 38–49.

Gaddes, W. H. (1980). *Learning disabilities and brain function.* New York: Springer-Verlag.

Gaddes. W. H. (1985). *Learning disabilities and brain function: A neuropsychological approach* (2nd ed.). New York: Springer-Verlag.

Galaburda, A. M., & Eidelberg, D. (1982). Symmetry and asymmetry in the human posterior thalamus. II. Thalamic lesions in a case of developmental dyslexia. *Archives of Neurology, 39,* 333–336.

Galaburda, A. M., & Kemper, T. L. (1979). Cytoarchitectonic abnormalities in developmental dyslexia: A case study. *Annals of Neurology, 6,* 94–100.

Galaburda, A. M., Sherman, G. F., Rosen, G. D., Aboitiz, F., & Geschwind, N. (1985). Developmental dyslexia: Four consecutive patients with cortical anomalies. *Annals of Neurology, 18,* 222–233.

Galton, F. (1892). *Hereditary geniuses* (2nd ed.). London: Macmillan.

Garron, D. C., & Cheifetz, D. I. (1965). Comment on "Bender Gestalt discernment of organic pathology." *Psychological Bulletin, 63,* 197–200.

Gazzaniga, M. S. (1975). Recent research on hemispheric lateralization of the human brain: Review of the split brain. *UCLA Educator, 17,* 9–12.

Geary, D. C., & Gilger, J. W. (1984). The Luria-Nebraska Neuropsychological Battery—Children's Revision: Comparison of Learning-disabled and normal children matched on full scale IQ. *Perceptual and Motor Skills, 58,* 115–118.

Geary, D. C., Jennings, S. M., Schultz, D. D., & Alper, T. G. (1984). The diagnostic accuracy of the Luria-Nebraska Neuropsychological Battery—Children's Revision for 9- to 12-year-old learning-disabled children. *School Psychology Review, 13,* 375–380.

Gelles, R. J. (1978). Violence toward children in the United States. *American Journal of Orthopsychiatry, 48,* 580.

Gerstmann, J. (1924). Fingeragnosie: Eine unschriebene störung der orientierung am eigherst körper. *Wein Klin. Wchnschr., 37,* 1010–1012.

Gerstmann, J. (1930). Zur symptomatologie der hirnlasionen im uebergangsgebiet der unteren parietal und mitteleren occipitalwindung. *Nervenarzt, 3,* 691–695.

Geschwind, N., & Behan, P. O. (1982). Left handedness: Association with immune disease, migraine, and developmental learning disorders. *Proceedings of the National Academy of Sciences, 79,* 5097–5100.

Geschwind, N., & Galaburda, A. M. (1985a). Cerebral lateralization: Biological mechanisms, associations, and pathology. I. A hypothesis and a program for research. *Archives of Neurology, 42,* 428–459.

Geschwind, N., & Galaburda, A. M. (1985b). Cerebral lateralization: Biological mechanisms, associations and pathology. II. A hypothesis and a program for research. *Archives of Neurology, 42,* 521–552.

Geschwind, N., & Galaburda, A. M. (1985c). Cerebral lateralization: Biological mechanisms, associations, and pathology. III. A hypothesis and a program for research. *Archives of Neurology, 42,* 634–654.

Geschwind, N., & Levitsky, W. (1968). Human brain: Left-right asymmetries in temporal speech region. *Science, 161,* 186–187.

Gilger, J. W., & Geary, D. C. (1985). Performance on the Luria-Nebraska Neuropsychological Test Battery—Children's Revision: A comparison of children with and without significant WISC—R VIQ-PIQ discrepancies. *Journal of Clinical Psychology, 41,* 806–811.

Goh, D. S., Teslow, C. J., & Fuller, G. B. (1980, April). The practice of psychological assessment among school psychologists. Paper presented at the twelfth annual convention of the National Association of School Psychologists. Washington, DC.

Golden, C. J. (1981). The Luria-Nebraska Children's Battery: Theory and formulation. In G. W. Hynd & J. E. Obrzut (Eds.), *Neuropsychological assessment and the school-age child: Issues and perspectives* (pp. 277–302). New York: Grune & Stratton.

Golden, C. J., Hammeke, T. A., & Purisch, A. D. (1978). Diagnostic validity of a standardized neuropsychological battery derived from Luria's neuropsychological tests. *Journal of Consulting and Clinical Psychology, 46*, 1258–1265.

Goldstein, K. (1970). Paul Broca. In W. Haymaker & F. Schiller (Eds.), *The founders of neurology* (2nd ed., pp. 12–16). Springfield, IL: Charles C Thomas, Publishers.

Gomez, M. R. (1967). Minimal cerebral dysfunction (maximal neurologic confusion). *Clinical Pediatrics, 6*, 589–591.

Greenblatt, S. H. (1965). The major influences on the early life and works of John Hughlings Jackson. *Bulletin of the History of Medicine, 39*, 346–376.

Greenblatt, S. H. (1977). The development of Hughlings Jackson's approach to diseases of the nervous system 1863–1866: Unilateral seizures, hemiplegia, and aphasia. *Bulletin of the History of Medicine, 51*, 412–430.

Gulbrandsen, G. B. (1984). Neuropsychological sequelae of light head injuries in older children six months after trauma. *Journal of Clinical Neuropsychology, 6*, 257–268.

Gustavson, J. L., Golden, C. J., Leark, R. A., Wilkening, G. N., Hermann, B. P., & Plaisted, J. R. (1982, August). The Luria-Nebraska Neuropsychological Battery—Children's Revision: Current research findings. Paper presented at the meeting of the American Psychological Association, Washington, DC.

Gustavson, J. L., Golden, C. J., Wilkening, G. N., Hermann, B. P., Plaisted, J. R., MacInnes, W. D., & Leark, R. A. (1984). The Luria-Nebraska Neuropsychological Battery-Children's Revision: Validation with brain-damaged and normal children. *Journal of Psychoeducational Assessment, 2*, 199–208.

Gustavson, J. L., Wilkening, G. N., Hermann, B. P., & Plaisted, J. R. (1982). Factor analysis of the children's revision of the Luria-Nebraska Neuropsychological Battery. Unpublished manuscript.

Halstead, W. C. (1947). *Brain and intelligence: A quantitative study of the frontal lobes.* Chicago: The University of Chicago Press.

Halstead, W. C. (1951). Biological intelligence. *Journal of Personality, 20*, 118–130.

Halstead, W. C., & Wepman, J. M. (1949). The Halstead-Wepman Aphasia Screening Test. *Journal of Speech and Hearing Disorders, 14*, 9–13.

Hammil, D. D., Leigh, J. E., McNutt, G., & Larsen, S. C. (1981). A new definition of learning disabilities. *Learning Disabilities Quarterly, 4*, 336–342.

Head, H. (1926). *Aphasia and kindred disorders of speech.* London: Cambridge University Press.

Hécaen, H., & Albert, M. C. (1978). *Human neuropsychology.* New York: Wiley.

Hécaen, H., & Piercy, M. (1956). Paroxysmal dysphasia and the problem of cerebral dominance. *Journal of Neurology, Neurosurgery, and Psychiatry, 19*, 194–201.

Heilman, K. M., & Valenstein, E. (1979). *Clinical neuropsychology.* New York: Oxford University Press.

Henderson, V. W. (1986). Paul Broca's less heralded contribution to aphasia research. *Archives of Neurology, 43*, 609–612.

Hermann, B. P. (1982a). Neuropsychological correlates of aggression in children with epilepsy. Unpublished manuscript.

Hermann, B. P. (1982b). Adequacy of neuropsychological functioning and psychopathology in children with epilepsy. Unpublished manuscript.

Hermann, K. (1964). Specific reading disability. *Danish Medical Bulletin, 11*, 34–40.

Hersher, L. (1978). Minimal brain dysfunction and otitis media. *Perceptual and Motor Skills, 47*, 723.

Hinshelwood, J. (1895). Word-blindness and visual memory. *Lancet, 2*, 1564–1570.

Hinshelwood, J. (1900). Congenital word-blindness. *Lancet, 1*, 1506–1508.

Hinshelwood, J. (1902). Congenital word-blindness, with reports of two cases. *Ophthalmic Review, 21*, 91–99.

Hinshelwood, J. (1909). Four cases of congenital word-blindness occurring in the same family. *British Medical Journal, 2*, 1229–1232.

Hirschenfang, S. A. (1960). A comparison of Bender Gestalt reproductions of right and left hemiplegic patients. *Journal of Clinical Psychology, 16*, 439.

Hooper, S., & Hynd, G. W. (1985). Differential diagnosis of subtypes of developmental dyslexia with the Kaufman Assessment Battery for Children (K-ABC). *Journal of Clinical Child Psychology, 14*, 145–152.

Horwood, S. P., Boyle, M. H., Torrance, G. W., & Sinclair, J. C. (1982). Mortality and morbidity of 500- to 1,499-gram birth weight infants live-born to residents of a defined geographic region before and after neonatal intensive care. *Pediatrics, 69*, 613–620.

Howie, V. M. (1977). Acute and recurrent otitis media. In B. Jaffe (Ed.), *Hearing loss in children* (pp. 23–47). Baltimore: University Park Press.

Hyman, L. M. (1983). *An investigation of the neuropsychological characteristics of learning-disabled children as measured by the Luria-Nebraska (Children).* (Doctoral dissertation, University of Southern California, 1983). *Dissertation Abstracts International, 44* (11-A), 3327.

Hynd, G. W., & Cohen, M. (1983). *Dyslexia: Neuropsychological theory, research, and clinical differentiation.* New York: Grune & Stratton.

Hynd, G. W., & Hynd, C. R. (1984). Dyslexia: Neuroanatomical/neurolinguistic perspectives. *Reading Research Quarterly, 19*, 482–498.

Hynd, G. W., Hynd, C. R., Sullivan, H. G., & Kingsbury, T., Jr. (1987). Regional cerebral blood flow (rCBF) in developmental dyslexics: Activation during reading in a surface and deep dyslexic. *Journal of Learning Disabilities, 20*, 294–300.

Hynd, G.W., Obrzut, J.E. (Eds.) (1981). *Neuropsychological assessment and the school-age child: Issues and procedures.* New York: Grune & Stratton, Inc.

Hynd, G. W., Obrzut, J. E., & Obrzut, A. (1981). Are lateral and perceptual asymmetries related to WISC—R and achievement test performance in normal and learning-disabled children? *Journal of Consulting and Clinical Psychology, 49*, 977–979.

Hynd, G. W., & Semrud-Clikeman, M. (1988). *Dyslexia and neurodevelopmental pathology: Relationships to cognition, intelligence and reading skill acquisition.* Manuscript submitted for publication.

Hynd, G. W., & Snow, J. H. (1986). Assessment of neurological and neuropsychological factors associated with severe learning disabilities. In D. J. Lazarus & S. S. Strichart (Eds.), *Psychoeducational evaluation of children with low incidence handicaps* (pp. 239–266). New York: Grune & Stratton, Inc.

Hynd, G. W., & Willis, W. G. (1985). Neurological foundations of intelligence. In B.
    B. Wolman (Ed.), *Handbook of intelligence* (pp. 119–158). New York: John Wiley
    & Sons.
Hynd, G. W., & Willis, W. G. (1988). *Pediatric neuropsychology.* Orlando, FL:
    Grune & Stratton, Inc.
Incagnoli, T., & Kane, R. (1983). Developmental perspective of the Gilles De La
    Tourette syndrome. *Perceptual and Motor Skills, 57,* 1271–1281.
Jellinger, J. (1972). Neuropathological features of unclassified mental retardation. In
    J. B. Cavanaugh (Ed.), *The brain in unclassified mental retardation.* Baltimore:
    Williams & Wilkins.
Johnson, D. J., & Myklebust, H. R. (1967). *Learning disabilities: Educational prin-
    ciples and practices.* New York: Grune & Stratton, Inc.
Kalsbeck, W. D., McLauren, R. L., Harris, B.S.H., III, & Miller, J. D. (1980). The
    national head and spinal cord injury survey: Major findings. *Journal of Neuro-
    surgery, 53,* 19–31.
Kamphaus, R. W., Kaufman, A. S., & Kaufman, N. L. (1982, August). A cross-
    validation study of sequential-simultaneous processing at ages 2½–12½ using the
    Kaufman Assessment Battery for Children (K-ABC). Paper presented at the
    annual convention of the American Psychological Association, Washington, DC.
Karras, D., Newlin, D. B., Franzen, M. D., Golden, C. J., Wilkening, G. N.,
    Rothermel, R. D., & Tramontana, M. J. (1987). Development of factor scales for
    the Luria-Nebraska Neuropsychological Battery—Children's Revision. *Journal of
    Clinical Child Psychology, 16,* 19–28.
Katz, J. (1978). The effects of conductive hearing loss on auditory function. *Journal of
    the American Speech and Hearing Association, 20,* 879.
Kaufman, A. S. (1979). *Intelligent testing with the WISC—R.* New York: Wiley Inter-
    science.
Kaufman, A. S. (1983). Intelligence: Old concepts—New perspectives. In G. W.
    Hynd (Ed.), *The school psychologist: An introduction* (pp. 95–118). Syracuse, NY:
    Syracuse University Press.
Kaufman, A. S., Kaufman, N. L., Kamphaus, R. W., & Naglieri, J. A. (1982).
    Sequential and simultaneous factors at ages 3–12½: Developmental changes in
    neuropsychological dimensions. *Clinical Neuropsychology, 4,* 74–81.
Kelly, J. P. (1985). Anatomical basis of sensory perception and motor coordination.
    In E. R. Kandel & J. H. Schwartz (Eds.), *Principles of neural science* (2nd ed., pp.
    222–243). New York: Elsevier.
Kimura, D. (1961). Cerebral dominance and the perception of verbal stimuli. *Canadian
    Journal of Psychology, 15,* 166–171.
Kinsbourne, M. (1970). The cerebral basis of lateral asymmetries in attention. *Acta
    Psychologica, 33,* 193–201.
Kinsbourne, M. (1988). Foreword. Pediatric neuropsychology. Orlando: Grune &
    Stratton, Inc.
Kinsbourne, M., & Hiscock, M. (1981). Cerebral lateralization and cognitive devel-
    opment: Conceptual and methodological issues. In G. W. Hynd & J. E. Obrzut
    (Eds.), *Neuropsychological assessment and the school-age child: Issues and pro-
    cedures* (pp. 125–166). New York: Grune & Stratton, Inc.
Kinsbourne, M., & Warrington, E. K. (1963). Development factors in reading and
    writing backwardness. *British Journal of Psychology, 54,* 145–156.

References   137

Kirk, S. A. (1963). Behavioral diagnosis and remediation of learning disabilities. In *Conference on exploration into the problems of the perceptually handicapped child.* Evanston, IL: Fund for the Perceptually Handicapped Child.

Kirk, S. A. (1972). *Educating exceptional children.* Boston: Houghton-Mifflin Company.

Kirshner, H. S., & Kistler, K. H. (1982). Aphasia after right thalamic hemorrhage. *Archives of Neurology, 39,* 667–669.

Klegas, R. C. (1983). The relationship between neuropsychological, cognitive, and behavioral assessment of brain functioning in children. *Clinical Neuropsychology, 5,* 28–32.

Klegas, R. C., & Fisher, L. P. (1981). A multiple criterion approach to the assessment of brain damage in children. *Clinical Neuropsychology, 3* (4), 6–11.

Klonoff, H., & Low, M. D. (1974). Disordered brain function in young children and early adolescents: Neuropsychological and electroencephalographic correlates. In R. M. Reitan & L. A. Davison (Eds.), *Clinical neuropsychology: Current status and applications* (pp. 121–165). New York: V. H. Winston & Sons.

Kløve, H. (1974). Validation studies in adult clinical neuropsychology. In R. M. Reitan & L. A. Davison (Eds.), *Clinical neuropsychology: Current status and applications.* (pp. 211–236). New York: V. H. Winston & Sons.

Knights, R. M., & Norwood, J. A. (1979). *A neuropsychological test battery for children.* Ottawa, Canada: Psychological Consultants.

Knights, R. M., & Ogilvie, R. M. (1967). *A comparison of test results from normal and brain-damaged children* (Res. Bull. No. 53). London-Ontario: University of Western Ontario.

Kolb, D., & Whishaw, I. Q. (1980). *Fundamentals of human neuropsychology.* San Francisco: W. H. Freeman.

Kopp, N., Michel, F., Carrier, H., Biron, A., & Duvillard, P. (1977). Étude de certaines asymétries hémisphériques du cerveau humain. *Journal of the Neurological Sciences, 34,* 349–363.

Koppitz, E. M. (1963). *The Bender-Gestalt Test for Young Children.* New York: Grune & Stratton, Inc.

Kraepelin, E. (1895). Der psychologische versuch in der psychiatrie. *Psychologische Arbeiten, 1,* 1–91.

Lahey, B. B., & Ciminero, A. R. (1980). *Maladaptive behavior: An introduction to abnormal psychology.* Glenview, IL: Scott, Foresman and Company.

Lashley, K. S. (1951). The problem of serial order in behavior. In L. A. Jeffres (Ed.), *Cerebral mechanisms in behavior* (pp. 112–136). New York: Wiley.

Leark, R. A., Gustavson, J. L., Wilkening, G. N., & Golden, C. J. (1982, October). *Relationship of WISC—R IQ scores to Luria-Nebraska Neuropsychological Battery-Children's Revision scales.* Paper presented at the meeting of the National Academy of Neuropsychologists, Orlando, FL.

Lenneberg, E. H. (1967). *Biological foundations of language.* New York: Wiley.

Lennox, W. G. (1970). Hughlings Jackson. In W. Haymaker & F. Schiller (Eds.), *The founders of neurology* (2nd ed., pp. 456–459). Springfield, IL: Charles C Thomas, Publishers.

Lezak, M. D. (1976). *Neuropsychological assessment.* New York: Oxford University Press.

Lindgren, S. D. (1978). Finger localization and the prediction of reading disability. *Cortex, 14,* 87–101.

Lombroso, C. T. (1967). Sylvian seizures and midtemporal spike foci in children. *Archives of Neurology, 17,* 52–59.

Lou, H. C., Henriksen, L., & Bruhn, P. (1984). Focal cerebral hypoperfusion in children with dysphasia and/or attention deficit disorder. *Archives of Neurology, 41,* 825–829.

Luria, A. R. (1970). Functional organization of the brain. *Scientific American, 222,* 66–78.

Luria, A. R. (1973). *The working brain: An introduction to neuropsychology.* New York: Basic Books.

Luria, A. R. (1980). *Higher cortical functions in man* (2nd ed.). New York: Basic Books.

Luria, A. R., & Majovski, L. V. (1977). Basic approaches used in American and Soviet clinical neuropsychology. *American Psychologist, 32,* 959–968.

Mackie, R. D. (1969). *Special education in the United States: Statistics 1946–1966.* New York: Teacher's College.

Malamud, N. (1964). Neuropathology. In H. A. Stevens & R. Heber (Eds.), *Mental retardation* (pp. 429–452). Chicago: University of Chicago Press.

Matuszek, P. (1985). Review of the Wide Range Achievement Test, 1978 edition. In J. V. Mitchell, Jr. (Ed.), *The ninth mental measurements yearbook* (pp. 1734–1736). Lincoln, NE: The University of Nebraska Press.

McCaffrey, R. J., Malloy, P. F., & Brief, D. J. (in press). Internship opportunities in clinical neuropsychology emphasizing recent INS training guidelines. *Professional Psychology: Research and Practice.*

McCarthy, M. (1975). Social aspects of treatment in childhood leukemia. *Social Science and Medicine, 9,* 263–269.

McFie, J. (1960). Psychological testing in clinical neurology. *Journal of Nervous and Mental Disease, 131,* 383–393.

McKay, S. E., Stelling, M. W., Baumann, R. J., Carr, W. A., Walsh, J. W., & Gilmore, R. L. (1985). Assessment of frontal lobe dysfunction using the Luria-Nebraska Neuropsychological Battery—Children's Revision: A case study. *International Journal of Clinical Neuropsychology, 7,* 23–27.

Milner, B. (1974). Hemispheric specialization: Scope and limits. In F. O. Schmitt & F. G. Worden (Eds.), *The neurosciences third study program* (pp. 75–89). Cambridge: MIT Press.

Mitchell, S. W., Morehouse, G., & Keen, W. W., Jr. (1864). *Reflex paralysis, article 6.* Washington, DC: Surgeon General's Office.

Morgan, W. P. (1896). A case of congenital word-blindness. *British Medical Journal, 2,* 1378.

Myklebust, H. R., & Boshes, B. (1969). *Final report, minimal brain damage in children.* Washington, DC: United States Department of Health, Education and Welfare.

Naeser, M. A., Alexander, M. P., Helm-Estabrooks, N., Levine, H. L., Laughlin, S. A., & Geschwind, N. (1982). Aphasia with predominantly subcortical lesion sites: Description of three capsular/putaminal aphasia syndromes. *Archives of Neurology, 39,* 2–14.

Needleman, H. (1977). Effects of hearing loss from early recurrent otitis media on speech and language development. In B. Jaffe (Ed.), *Hearing loss in children.* Baltimore, MD: University Park Press.

Nickel, R. E., Bennett, F. C., & Lamson, F. F. (1982). School performance of children with birth weights of 1,000 g. or less. *American Journal of Diseases of Children, 136*, 105–110.

Nolan, D. R., Hammeke, T. A., & Barkley, R. A. (1983). A comparison of the patterns of the neuropsychological performance in two groups of learning-disabled children. *Journal of Clinical Child Psychology, 12*, 13–21.

O'Leary, D. S., Lovell, M. R., Sackellares, J. C., Berent, S., Giordani, B., Seidenberg, M., & Boll, T. J. (1983). Effects of age of onset of partial & generalized seizures on neuropsychological performance in children. *Journal of Nervous and Mental Disease, 171*, 624–629.

Obrzut, J. E. (1981). Neuropsychological procedures with school-age children. In G. W. Hynd & J. E. Obrzut (Eds.), *Neuropsychological assessment and the school-age child: Issues and procedures* (pp. 237–275). New York: Grune & Stratton, Inc.

Obrzut, J. E., Hynd, G. W., & Obrzut, A. (1983). Neuropsychological assessment of learning disabilities: A discriminant analysis. *Journal of Experimental Child Psychology, 35* (1), 46–55.

Oldfield, R. C. (1971). The assessment and analysis of handedness: The Edinburgh Handedness Inventory. *Neuropsychologia, 9*, 97–113.

Orzeck, A. Z. (1966). *The Orzeck Aphasia Evaluation*. Los Angeles: Western Psychological Services.

Parsons, O. A., Vega, A., & Burn, J. (1969). Different psychological effects of lateralized brain damage. *Journal of Clinical and Consulting Psychology, 33*, 551–557.

Passler, M. A., Isaac, W., & Hynd, G. W. (1985). Neuropsychological development of behavior attributed to frontal lobe functions in children. *Developmental Neuropsychology, 1*, 349–370.

Penfield, W., & Roberts, L. (1959). *Speech and brain mechanisms*. Princeton, NJ: Princeton University Press.

Pirozzolo, F. J. (1979). *The neuropsychology of developmental reading disorders*. New York: Praeger Publishers.

Plaisted, J. R., Gustavson, J. L., Wilkening, G. N., & Golden, C. J. (1983). The Luria-Nebraska Neuropsychological Battery—Children's Revision: Theory and current research findings. *Journal of Clinical Child Psychology, 12*, 13–21.

Putnam, J. J. (1875). Wernecke on the theory of aphasia. *Boston Medical and Surgical Journal*, 583–587.

Quattrocchi, M. M., & Golden, C. J. (1983). Peabody Picture Vocabulary Test—Revised and Luria-Nebraska Neuropsychological Battery for Children: Intercorrelations for normal youngsters. *Perceptual and Motor Skills, 56*, 632–634.

Quercy, M. (1943). Les fondateurs de la doctrine française de l'aphasie. *Annales Medico-Psychologiques, 2*, 162–188.

Rao, K.C.V.G., & Kishore, P.R.S. (1984). Neuroradiology in pediatric emergencies. In J. M. Pellock & E. C. Myer (Eds.), *Neurologic emergencies in infancy and childhood* (pp. 349–389). Philadelphia: Harper & Row Publishers.

Reed, H.B.C. (1976). Pediatric neuropsychology. *Journal of Pediatric Psychology, 1*, 5–7.

Reed, H.B.C., Reitan, R. M., & Kløve, H. (1965). Influence of cerebral lesions on psychological test performances of older children. *Journal of Consulting Psychology, 29*, 247–251.

Reitan, R. M. (1955). Certain differential effects of left and right cerebral lesions in human adults. *Journal of Comparative Physiological Psychology, 48*, 474.

Reitan, R. M. (1964). Psychological deficits resulting from cerebral lesions in man. In J. M. Warren & K. A. Akert (Eds.), *The frontal granular cortex and behavior* (pp. 23–67). New York: McGraw-Hill.

Reitan, R. M. (1966). Diagnostic inferences of brain lesions based on psychological test results. *Canadian Psychologist, 7*, 386–392.

Reitan, R. M. (1971a). Sensorimotor functions in brain-damaged and normal children of early school age. *Perceptual and Motor Skills, 33*, 655–664.

Reitan, R. M. (1971b). Trail-Making Test results for normal and brain-damaged children. *Perceptual and Motor Skills, 33*, 575–581.

Reitan, R. M. (1974). Psychological effects of cerebral lesions in children of early school age. In R. M. Reitan & L. A. Davison (Eds.), *Clinical neuropsychology: Current status and application* (pp. 53–90). New York: V. H. Winston & Sons.

Reitan, R. M. (1980). Applications of neuropsychological testing in psychiatric diagnosis. Unpublished manuscript.

Reitan, R. M., & Boll, T. J. (1973). Neuropsychological correlates of minimal brain dysfunction. *Annals of the New York Academy of Sciences, 205*, 65–88.

Reitan, R. M., & Davison, L. A. (1974). *Clinical neuropsychology: Current status and applications.* New York: V. H. Winston & Sons.

Reynolds, C. R. (1981). The neuropsychological basis of intelligence. In G. W. Hynd & J. E. Obrzut (Eds.), *Neuropsychological assessment and the school-age child: Issues and procedures* (pp. 87–124). New York: Grune & Stratton, Inc.

Riese, W. (1950). *Principles of neurology.* New York: Coolidge Foundation Publishers.

Rosen, G. D., & Galaburda, A. M. (1984). Development of language: A question of asymmetry and deviation. In J. Mehler & R. Fox (Eds.), *Neonate cognition: Beyond the blooming buzzing confusion.* Hillsdale, NJ: Lawrence Erlbaum Associates, Inc.

Ross, A. O. (1976). *Psychological aspects of learning disabilities and reading disorders.* New York: McGraw-Hill.

Rourke, B. P. (1975). Brain-behavior relationships in children with learning disabilities. A research program. *American Psychologist, 30*, 911–920.

Rourke, B. P. (1976). Issues in the neuropsychological assessment of children with learning disabilities. *Canadian Psychological Review, 17*, 89–102.

Rourke, B. P., & Finlayson, M.A.J. (1975). Neuropsychological significance of variation in patterns of performance on the Trail-Making Test for older children with learning disabilities. *Journal of Abnormal Psychology, 84* (4), 412–421.

Rourke, B. P., & Finlayson, M.A.J. (1978). Neuropsychological significance of variations in patterns of academic performance: Verbal and visual-spatial abilities. *Journal of Abnormal Child Psychology, 6* (1), 121–133.

Rourke, B. P., & Gates, R. D. (1981). Neuropsychological research and school psychology. In G. W. Hynd & J. E. Obrzut (Eds.), *Neuropsychological assessment of the school-age child: Issues and procedures* (pp. 3–25). New York: Grune & Stratton.

Rourke, B. P., & Telegdy, G. A. (1971). Laterlizing significance of WISC verbal-performance discrepancies for older children with learning disabilities. *Perceptual and Motor Skills, 33*, 875–883.

Rourke, B. P., Young, G. C., & Flewelling, R. W. (1971). The relationship between

WISC verbal-performance discrepancies and selective verbal, auditory-perceptual, visual-perceptual, and problem solving abilities in children with learning disabilities. *Journal of Clinical Psychology, 27*, 475–479.

Rubens, A. B., Mahuwald, M. W., & Hutton, J. T. (1976). Asymmetry of the lateral (sylvian) fissures in man. *Neurology, 26*, 620–624.

Rugel, R. P. (1974). WISC subtest scores of disabled readers: A review with respect to Bannatyne's recategorization. *Journal of Learning Disabilities, 7*, 48–55.

Rutter, M., Tizard, J., & Whitmore, K. (Eds.). (1970). *Education, health and behavior.* London: Longmans.

Saigh, D. A. (1985). Review of Wide Range Achievement Test, 1978 edition. In J. V. Mitchell, Jr. (Ed.), *The ninth mental measurements yearbook* (p. 1736). Lincoln, NE: The University of Nebraska Press.

Satz, P. (1976). Cerebral dominance and reading disability: An old problem revisited. In R. M. Knights & D. J. Bakker (Eds.), *The neuropsychology of learning disorders: Theoretical approaches* (pp. 273–294). Baltimore: University Park Press.

Satz, P., & Bullard-Bates, C. (1981). Acquired aphasia in children. In M. T. Sarno (Ed.), *Acquired aphasia* (pp. 399–429). New York: Academic Press.

Satz, P., & Fletcher, J. M. (1981). Emergent trends in neuropsychology: An overview. *Journal of Consulting and Clinical Psychology, 49*, 851–865.

Satz, P., & Friel, J. (1973). Some predictive antecedents of specific learning disability: A preliminary one-year follow-up. In P. Satz & J. Ross (Eds.), *The disabled learner.* Rotterdam: Rotterdam University Press.

Satz, P., Orsini, D. L., Saslow, E., & Henry, R. (1985). The pathological left-handedness syndrome. *Brain and Language, 4*, 27–46.

Satz, P., & Soper, H. V. (1986). Left-handedness, dyslexia and auto immune disorder: A critique. *Journal of Clinical and Experimental Neuropsychology, 8*, 453–458.

Satz, P., & Strauss, E. (1986, June). The ontogeny of hemispheric specialization: Some old hypotheses revisited. Paper presented at the Rodin Conference, King's College, University of Cambridge.

Satz, P., Taylor, H. G., Friel, J., & Fletcher, J. (1978). Some developmental and predictive precursors of reading disabilities: A six-year follow-up. In A. L. Benton & D. Pearl (Eds.), *Dyslexia: An appraisal of current knowledge* (pp. 313–347). New York: Oxford University Press.

Sawicki, R. F., Leark, R., Golden, C. J., & Karras, D. (1984). The development of the pathognomonic, left sensorimotor, and right sensorimotor scales for the Luria-Nebraska Neuropsychological Battery—Children's Revision. *Journal of Clinical Child Psychology, 13* (2), 165–169.

Schaughency, E. A., Lahey, B. B., Hynd, G. W., Stone, P. A., & Piacentini, J. C. (1988). Neuropsychological test performance and the attention-deficit disorders. *Journal of Consulting and Clinical Psychology* (in press).

Schiller, F. (1970). Franz Gall. In W. Haymaker & F. Schiller (Eds.), *The founders of neurology* (2nd ed., pp. 31–34). Springfield, IL: Charles C Thomas, Publishers.

Schurr, P. H. (1979). Head injuries. In F. C. Rose (Ed.), *Paediatric neurology* (pp. 497–508). Oxford: Blackwell Scientific Publishers.

Seidenberg, M., Giordani, B., Berent, S., Boll, T. J. (1983). IQ level and performance on the Halstead-Reitan Neuropsychological Test Battery for Older Children. *Journal of Consulting and Clinical Psychology, 51* (3), 406–413.

Selz, M. (1977). A neuropsychological model of learning disability: Classification of brain function in 9- to 14-year-old children. Unpublished doctoral dissertation, University of Washington.

Selz, M. (1981). Halstead-Reitan Neuropsychological Test Batteries for Children. In G. W. Hynd & J. E. Obrzut (Eds.), *Neuropsychological assessment and the school-age child: Issues and procedures* (pp. 195–235). New York: Grune & Stratton, Inc.

Selz, M., & Reitan, R. M. (1979a). Rules for neuropsychological diagnosis: Classification of brain function in older children. *Journal of Consulting and Clinical Psychology, 47* (2), 258–264.

Selz, M., & Reitan, R. M. (1979b). Neuropsychological test performance of normal, learning-disabled, and brain-damaged older children. *Journal of Nervous and Mental Disease, 167* (5), 298–302.

Sherman, G. F., Galaburda, A. M., & Geschwind, N. (in press). "Dyslexic" abnormalities in the brain of the autoimmune mouse. *Science.*

Sherrets, S., Quattrocchi, M., & Menolascino, F. (1982). Psychological and neuropsychological findings in a child with supravalvular aortic stenosis (William's Syndrome). *Clinical Neuropsychology, 4,* 186–190.

Silverberg, R., & Gordon, H. W. (1979). Differential aphasia in two bilingual individuals. *Neurology, 29,* 51–55.

Smith, F. (1982). *Understanding reading* (3rd ed.). New York: Holt, Rinehart, & Winston.

Snow, J. H., Hartlage, L. C., Hynd, G. W., & Grant, D. H. (1983). The relationship between the Luria-Nebraska Neuropsychological Battery—Children's Revision and the Minnesota Percepto-Diagnostic Test with learning-disabled students. *Psychology in the Schools, 20,* 415–419.

Snow, J. H., & Hynd, G. W. (1985a). Factor structure of the Luria-Nebraska Neuropsychological Battery—Children's Revision. *Journal of School Psychology, 23,* 271–276.

Snow, J. H., & Hynd, G. W. (1985b). A multivariate investigation of the Luria-Nebraska Neuropsychological Battery—Children's Revision with learning-disabled children. *Journal of Psychoeducational Assessment, 3,* 101–109.

Snow, J. H., Hynd, G. W., & Hartlage, L. C. (1984). Difference between mildly and more severely learning-disabled children on the Luria-Nebraska Neuropsychological Battery—Children's Revision. *Journal of Psychoeducational Assessment, 2,* 23–28.

Snyder, T. J., Leark, R. A., Golden, C. J., Grove, T., & Allison, R. (1983, March). *Correlation of the K-ABC, WISC—R, and Luria-Nebraska Children's Battery for Exceptional Children.* Paper presented at the meeting of the National Association of School Psychologists, Detroit, MI.

Sperry, R. W. (1964). The great cerebral commissure. *Scientific American, 210,* 240–250.

Spiers, P. A. (1982). Have they come to praise Luria or to bury him?: The Luria-Nebraska battery controversy. *Journal of Consulting and Clinical Psychology, 49,* 331–341.

Spitzka, E. C. (1882). Editorial notes and comments: The Guiteau autopsy. *American Journal of Neurology and Psychiatry, 1,* 381–392.

Spreen, O., & Benton, A. L. (1977). *Neurosensory center comprehensive examination for aphasia.* Victoria, B.C.: Department of Psychology, University of Victoria.

Spreen, O., & Gaddes, W. H. (1969). Developmental norms for 15 neuropsychological tests age 6 to 15. *Cortex, 5,* 171–191.

Springer, S. P., & Deutsch, G. (1981). *Left brain, right brain.* San Francisco: W. H. Freeman and Company.

Stambrook, M. (1983). The Luria-Nebraska Neuropsychological Battery: A promise that may be partly fulfilled. *International Journal of Clinical Neuropsychology, 5,* 247–269.

Stone, J. C., & Schneider, F. W. (1965). *Foundations of education.* New York: Thomas Y. Crowell Company.

Stores, G. (1978). School-children with epilepsy at risk for learning and behavior problems. *Developmental Medicine and Child Neurology, 20,* 502–508.

Stores, G., & Hart, J. (1976). Reading skills of children with generalized or focal epilepsy attending ordinary school. *Developmental Medicine and Child Neurology, 18,* 705–716.

Strom, D. A., Gray, J. W., Dean, R. S., & Fischer, W. E. (1987). The incremental validity of the Halstead-Reitan Neuropsychological Battery in predicting achievement for learning-disabled children. *Journal of Psychoeducational Assessment, 2,* 157–165.

Sutter, E. G., Bishop, P. G., & Battin, R. R. (1986). Factor similarities between traditional psychoeducational and neuropsychological test batteries. *Journal of Psychoeducational Assessment, 4,* 73–82.

Swiercinsky, D. P. (1979). Factorial pattern description and comparison of functional abilities in neuropsychological assessment. *Perceptual and Motor Skills, 48,* 231–241.

Taylor, H. G., Fletcher, J. M., & Satz, P. (1982). Component processes in reading disabilities: Neuropsychological investigation of distinct subskill deficits. In R. N. Malatesha & P. G. Aaron (Eds.), *Reading disorders: Varieties and treatments* (pp. 121–147). New York: Academic Press.

Taylor, H. G., Fletcher, J. M., & Satz, P. (1984). Neuropsychological assessment of children. In M. Hersen & G. Goldstein (Eds.), *Handbook of psychological assessment.* New York: Pergamon Press.

Taylor, J. (Ed.). (1956). *Selected writings of John Hughlings Jackson.* New York: Basic Books, Inc.

Teeter, P. A. (1983). The relationship between measures of cognitive-intellectual and neuropsychological abilities for young children. *Clinical Neuropsychology, 5* (4), 151–158.

Teeter, P. A. (1985). Neurodevelopmental investigation of academic achievement. A report of years 1 and 2 of a longitudinal study. *Journal of Consulting and Clinical Psychology, 53,* 709–717.

Teszner, D., Tzavaras, A., Gruner, J., & Hécaen, H. (1972). L'asymétrie droite-gauche du planum temporale; à propos de l'étude anatomique de 100 cerveaux. *Revue Neurologique, 126,* 444–449.

Townes, B. D., Reitan, R. M., & Trupin, E. W. (1978). Concept formation ability in brain-damaged & normal children. *Academic Therapy, 13,* 517–526.

Townes, B. D., Trupin, E. W., Martin, D. C., & Goldstein, D. (1980). Neuropsychological correlates of academic success among elementary school children. *Journal of Consulting and Clinical Psychology, 48,* 675–684.

Tramontana, M. G., & Hooper, S. (1988). *Neuropsychological assessment with children.* New York: Plenum Press.

144   NEUROPSYCHOLOGICAL ASSESSMENT IN CLINICAL CHILD PSYCHOLOGY

Tramontana, M. G., Klee, S. H., Boyd, T. A. (1984). WISC—R interrelationships with the Halstead-Reitan and Children's Luria Neuropsychological Batteries. *The International Journal of Clinical Neuropsychology, 6* (1), 1–8.

Tramontana, M. G., Sherrets, S. D., Wolf, B. A. (1983). Comparability of the Luria-Nebraska & Halstead-Reitan neuropsychological batteries for older children. *The International Journal of Clinical Neuropsychology, 5* (4), 186–190.

Tshushima, W. T., & Towne, W. S. (1977). Neuropsychological abilities of young children with questionable brain damage. *Journal of Consulting and Clinical Psychology, 45,* 757–762.

Tuma, J. M., & Pratt, J. M. (1982). Clinical child psychology practice and training: A national survey. *Journal of Clinical Child Psychology, 11,* 27–34.

Ukhtomskii, A. A. (1945). *Essays on the physiology of the nervous system. Collected works* (vol. 4). Leningrad.

Von Monakov, C. V. (1911). Lokalization der hirnfunktionen. *Journal für Psychologie and Neurologie, 17,* 185–200.

Von Monakov, C. (1914). *Lokalisation im Grosshirn.*

Wada, J. A., Clarke, R., & Hamm, A. (1975). Cerebral hemispheric asymmetry in humans: Cortical speech zones in 100 adults and 100 infant brains. *Archives of Neurology, 32,* 239–246.

Walsh, A. A. (1985). Phrenology applied: The trial and conviction of Major Mitchell. *Communique, 13,* 3–4.

Ward, J. D. (1985). Central nervous system trauma. In J. M. Pellock & E. C. Myer (Eds.), *Neurologic emergencies in infancy and childhood* (pp. 107–122). Philadelphia: Harper & Row, Publishers.

Weinstein, E. A. (1984). Cerebral localization in 19th century America. *Brain and Cognition, 3,* 357–369.

Wender, P. (1974). Some speculations concerning a possible biochemical basis of minimal brain dysfunction. *Life Science, 14,* 1605–1621.

Whitaker, H. (1981, May). *Electrical stimulation studies of the language regions of the brain.* Presentation to the GRECC Clinical Conference, V.A. Medical Center, Minneapolis.

Wilkening, G. N., Golden, C. J., MacInnes, W. D., Plaisted, J. R., & Hermann, B. P. (1981, August). The Luria-Nebraska Neuropsychological Battery—Children's Revision: A preliminary report. Paper presented at the meeting of the American Psychological Association, Los Angeles, CA.

Willis, W. G., & Widerstrom, A. H. (1986). Structure and function in prenatal and postnatal neuropsychological development: A dynamic interaction. In J. E. Obrzut & G. W. Hynd (Eds.), *Child neuropsychology: Vol. I. Theory and research* (pp. 13–53). Orlando, FL: Academic Press.

Wilson, R. M. (1981). *Diagnostic and remedial reading: For classroom and clinic* (4th ed.). Columbus: Charles E. Merrill Publishing Company.

Winogran, H. W., Knights, R. M., & Bawden, H. N. (1984). Neuropsychological deficits following head injury in children. *Journal of Clinical Neuropsychology, 6,* 269–286.

Witelson, S. F., Pallie, W. (1973). Left hemisphere specialization for language in the newborn: Neuroanatomical evidence of asymmetry. *Brain, 96,* 641–646.

Wolf, B. A., & Tramontana, M. G. (1982). Aphasia Screening Test interrelationships with complete Halstead-Reitan test results for older children. *Clinical Neuropsychology, 4,* 179–186.

Wolf, M. (1986). Rapid alternating stimulus naming in the developmental dyslexias. *Brain and Language, 27*, 360–379.

Wolf, M., Bally, H., & Morris, R. (1986). Automaticity, retrieval processes, and reading: A longitudinal study in average and impaired readers. *Child Development, 57*, 988–1000.

Woods, B. T. (1980). The restricted effects of right hemisphere lesions after age one: Wechsler test data. *Neuropsychologia, 18*, 65–70.

Woods, B. T., & Carey, S. (1979). Language deficits after apparent clinical recovery from childhood aphasia. *Annals of Neurology, 6*, 405.

Yakovlev, P. I. (1970). Constantin von Monakow. In W. Haymaker & F. Schiller (Eds.), *The founders of neurology* (2nd ed., pp. 484–488). Springfield, IL: Charles C Thomas, Publishers.

Zaidel, E. (1976). Auditory vocabulary of the right hemisphere following brain bisection or hemidecortication. *Cortex, 12*, 191–211.

Zametkin, A. J., & Rapoport, J. L. (1986). The pathophysiology of attention-deficit disorder with hyperactivity: A review. In B. B. Lahey & A. Kazdin (Eds.), *Advances in clinical child psychology* (vol. 9). New York: Plenum Press.

Zangwill, O. L. (1960). *Cerebral dominance and its relation to psychological function.* Edinburgh: Oliver & Boyd.

Zangwill, O. L. (1984). Henry Hécaen and the origins of the International Neuropsychological Society. *Neuropsychologia, 22*, 813–815.

Zinkus, P. W., Gottlieb, M. I., & Schapiro, M. (1978). Developmental and psychoeducational sequelae of chronic otitis media. *American Journal of Diseases of Childhood, 132*, 1110.

SUBJECT INDEX

ABOUT THE AUTHOR

George W. Hynd is a Research Professor of Psychology and Educational Psychology at the University of Georgia and an Assistant Clinical Professor of Neurology at the Medical College of Georgia. He received his doctorate in psychology from the University of Northern Colorado and completed a post-doctoral fellowship in clinical neuropsychology at the Minneapolis VA Medical Center. He has authored or edited six books in the area of child/pediatric neuropsychology and has written numerous chapters and articles focusing on issues in child neuropsychology, learning disabilities, and childhood psychopathology. In addition to completing a Fulbright Fellowship in child neuropsychology in Finland, he is the Director of the Center for Clinical and Developmental Neuropsychology at the University of Georgia.

NOTES